KINDLE FIRE
QuickSteps®

JOLI BALLEW

New York Chicago San Francisco
Lisbon London Madrid Mexico City
Milan New Delhi San Juan
Seoul Singapore Sydney Toronto

The McGraw·Hill Companies

Cataloging-in-Publication Data is on file with the Library of Congress

KINDLE FIRE QUICKSTEPS®

1234567890   QDB QDB   1098765432

ISBN   978-0-07-179524-1
MHID   0-07-179524-3

SPONSORING EDITOR / Megg Morin

EDITORIAL SUPERVISOR / Patty Mon

PROJECT MANAGER / Tania Andrabi, Cenveo Publisher Services

ACQUISITIONS COORDINATOR / Stephanie Evans

TECHNICAL EDITOR / James Truscott

COPY EDITOR / Lisa McCoy

PROOFREADER / Susie Elkind

INDEXER / Ted Laux

PRODUCTION SUPERVISOR / Jean Bodeaux

COMPOSITION / Cenveo Publisher Services

ILLUSTRATION / Cenveo Publisher Services

ART DIRECTOR, COVER / Jeff Weeks

COVER DESIGNER / Pattie Lee

SERIES CREATORS / Marty and Carole Matthews

SERIES DESIGN / Bailey Cunningham

I am thankful for my family, Dad, Jennifer, Cosmo, and Andrew, and appreciate all they do!

About the Author

Joli Ballew is an award-winning, best-selling author of 40+ computer books. Joli has been working with computers, gadgets, and all things media since her freshman year in college in 1982, where she majored in computer science, then systems analysis, and finally mathematics. Ultimately, she earned her degree in the latter. Joli has written several books related to phones and mobile technologies, including the extremely popular *How to Do Everything: iPad 2* (McGraw-Hill, 2011) and *How to Do Everything: BlackBerry Storm 2* (McGraw-Hill, 2010). Joli also teaches computer classes at various colleges in the Dallas area and is the Microsoft IT Academy Coordinator at Brookhaven Community College in Farmers Branch, Texas.

Beyond writing books and teaching classes, Joli is a Microsoft MVP (five years running) and holds multiple Microsoft certifications, including Microsoft Certified Trainer. She studies new technologies regularly, and attends both the Consumer Electronics Show and the Microsoft MVP Summit every year. In her spare time, Joli exercises at the local gym, works outside tending to her lawn, and serves as the butler for her two cats, Pico and Lucy, and their pet gerbil, George.

You can contact Joli at Joli_Ballew@hotmail.com, and she welcomes your correspondence.

About the Technical Editor

James Truscott (MCSE, MCPI, Network+) has extensive technical experience in many fields. James' passion for computers started back in the 1970s when he was a programmer for Bell Telephone. Over the years he has been a beta tester for many products, including new programs, VoIP telephones, and several hardware products, including cell phones. In 2000, he taught MCSE (Microsoft Certified Systems Engineer) classes at Eastfield College and the Dallas County Community College District; later he was the senior instructor for the Cowell Corporation teaching SBC (Southwestern Bell Corporation) employees how to employ remote access on encrypted laptops. He has served as webmaster for Cowell Corporation and is currently a website contributor for the city of Garland, Texas. James also does consulting work for several Dallas-based businesses. Over the years he has been the technical editor for many technical books and articles, including the MCSE series from Syngress Books. In fact, James edited Joli Ballew's very first book, *Windows 2000 Professional* (McGraw-Hill, 2000). James is currently busy creating the next must-have iPhone app, and works for the city of Garland in various capacities.

Contents at a Glance

Contents

6

7

Chapter 8   Surfing the Web with Amazon Silk 141

Chapter 9   Using the Kindle Fire at Home, for Business, and for Travel 159

Chapter 10 **Managing, Maintaining, and Troubleshooting Your Kindle Fire** 181

Acknowledgments

This book is a team effort of truly talented people.

Megg Morin, sponsoring editor, project editor, friend, and Kindle Fire enthusiast. Megg hired me once again to write another mobile device book, and kept everyone in line, on track, and on time. Megg was always available (at least when she wasn't walking marathons), which is very important when pushing out a book so quickly and on such a tight schedule.

James Truscott, technical editor, who meticulously read and corrected my work, and did so quickly and precisely. James is a good friend, too, perhaps complicating the issue of having to be the bad guy every now and again.

Tania Andrabi, project manager, who coordinated the copyediting, proofreading, and layout and made sure all the right details got to the right spot.

Patty Mon helped us make sure the book looked just the way we wanted it to on each page.

Stephanie Evans helped to keep track of all the moving parts on the project.

Neil Salkind, my agent and friend, who goes out of his way to keep me busy. He's a great guy and my biggest fan. I'm sure I wouldn't be where I am today without him.

Erica Sadun and Liz Castro, two ladies I found on the Internet who helped me figure out how to take a screen shot of the Kindle Fire. Erica has a blog called TheFireBlog, should you like to visit it. It's all about the Kindle Fire.

My family, who has always supported my work and is finally reaping the benefits through royalties and weekends off!

Introduction

QuickSteps® books are recipe books for computer users. They answer the question "How do I...?" by providing quick sets of steps to accomplish the most common tasks in a particular program. The sets of steps are the central focus of the book. QuickSteps sidebars show you how to quickly do many small functions or tasks that support the primary functions. Notes, Tips, and Cautions augment the steps, yet they are presented in such a manner as to not interrupt the flow of the steps. The brief introductions are minimal rather than narrative, and numerous illustrations and figures, many with callouts, support the steps.

QuickSteps® books are organized by function and the tasks needed to perform that function. Each function is a chapter. Each task, or "How To," contains the steps needed for accomplishing the function along with relevant Notes, Tips, Cautions, and screenshots. Tasks will be easy to find through:

- The table of contents, which lists the functional areas (chapters) and tasks in the order they are presented

- A How-To list of tasks on the opening page of each chapter

- The index with its alphabetical list of terms used in describing the functions and tasks

- Color-coded tabs for each chapter or functional area, with an index to the tabs just before the table of contents

Conventions Used in This Book

Kindle Fire QuickSteps® uses several conventions designed to make the book easier for you to follow:

- A 🔍 or a 🎨 in the table of contents or the How-To list in each chapter references a QuickSteps or a QuickFacts sidebar in a chapter.

- **Bold type** is used for words on the screen that you are to do something with, such as click **Save As** or open **File**.

- *Italic type* is used for a word or phrase that is being defined or otherwise deserves special emphasis.

- Underlined type is used for text that you are to type from the keyboard.

- SMALL CAPITAL LETTERS are used for keys on the keyboard such as ENTER and SHIFT.

- When you are expected to enter a command, you are told to tap the key(s). If you are to enter text or numbers, you are told to type them. Specific letters or numbers to be entered will be underlined.

How to...

Chapter 1
Getting Started

Amazon offers various models of the Kindle e-book reader. There's the basic Kindle, the Kindle Touch, the Kindle Keyboard, and the Kindle DX. These models were created specifically to enable users to obtain and read electronic books, and there were a few experimental features included for those who wanted more. Those features included a way to receive email, access text-to-speech capabilities, copy and then play MP3s, and even surf the Web. However, these earlier Kindles could never be considered *tablet computers.* That's all over now, with the new Kindle Fire.

The Kindle Fire is a real tablet computer. You can personalize it; obtain and use apps; obtain and read books, newspapers, and magazines; and even watch movies and listen to music. You can play games; stream, rent, or buy movies from Amazon; surf the Internet with a relatively full web browser;

and enjoy the color touchscreen. You even get free "cloud" storage for the media you buy from Amazon.

Set Up Your Kindle Fire

Unless you received the Kindle Fire as a gift, it should be ready to use out of the box, registered to your Amazon account. All you have to do is input your time zone and, if applicable, your network's Wi-Fi password. If you received the Kindle Fire as a gift, you need to input your Amazon account information yourself.

Unpack the Kindle Fire

First, take your Kindle Fire out of the box and lay out the contents on a table. Set the packing materials aside. You should have received the following:

- The Kindle Fire
- Power adapter
- Quick Start Guide

Note that you will *not* receive a Universal Serial Bus (USB) cable to connect your Kindle Fire to your computer, so there's no need to look for it under the cardboard packaging! Once you're sure everything you need is included, continue on.

Turn On and Set Up Your Kindle Fire

To start the setup process, press the power button to turn on your Kindle Fire. The power button is located at the bottom of the device, in the middle, if you're holding it upright (in portrait mode), facing you. You'll see a screen with the time and an orange arrow on it. Slide that arrow from right to left to unlock the screen.

If the device won't turn on, you'll need to charge your Kindle Fire.

1. Connect the power adapter to the Kindle Fire. It connects at the bottom of the device when holding it upright in portrait mode, facing you.
2. Plug the power adapter into an outlet.
3. Wait while the device charges.

NOTE

If the Kindle Fire won't power on, you'll need to charge it. It can take up to four hours for the Kindle Fire to fully charge.

CAUTION

Although Amazon itself does not place any restrictions on the number of devices you can register with them (and to your account), publishers of content will place limits on how many devices you can "authorize" or "register" to access the content you buy. Thus, always deregister unwanted, lost, sold, or damaged devices if you're sure you won't use them anymore.

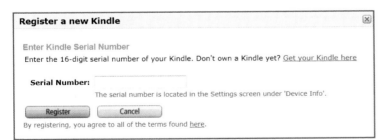

Register a new Kindle

Enter Kindle Serial Number
Enter the 16-digit serial number of your Kindle. Don't own a Kindle yet? <u>Get your Kindle here</u>

Serial Number:
              The serial number is located in the Settings screen under 'Device Info'.

Register   Cancel

By registering, you agree to all of the terms found <u>here</u>.

*Figure 1-1: **The Kindle Fire's serial number identifies it to Amazon.***

The first time you power on your Kindle Fire:

1. Swipe the orange arrow from right to left to unlock the screen.
2. If the Kindle Fire finds any Wi-Fi networks, it will list them. Tap your Wi-Fi network's name in the list if it is displayed. If it isn't listed, you'll have to enter the information manually, as outlined later in this chapter. You can also opt to skip this step and the next.
3. Type the network's Wi-Fi password and tap **Connect**.
4. Tap your time zone.
5. If prompted, enter your Amazon account information. If information is already input and it's correct, do nothing. If the incorrect account is listed, tap **Not <name>?** and input the correct information.
6. Wait for any updates to install and for the Kindle to complete the startup tasks.
7. The next time you move the slider, work through the short tutorial, tapping **Next** as prompted.

Register Your Kindle Fire Using a Computer

Your Kindle Fire should recognize you the moment you move the slider to unlock the screen. In almost all cases, even if you received the device as a gift, you'll still be able to set it up as outlined in the previous section, by inputting your Amazon account information manually. However, there may be rare instances when this doesn't work. If, for whatever reason, you can't register your Kindle Fire from the device itself, you can register it using a computer.

To register a Kindle Fire manually (or to register any other Kindle Fire device):

1. From your computer, log on to www.amazon.com using your personal Amazon account.
2. Click **Your Account** at the top of the page.
3. Scroll down and click **Manage Your Kindle**. Type your password.
4. If you don't see your Kindle Fire listed on this page, click **Register A Kindle**.
5. Type the serial number in the box provided. See Figure 1-1.

Explore the Controls and Home Screen

Now that your Kindle Fire is charged, powered on, and registered, you're ready to explore the external controls and the items on the Home screen. There's not much to the outside of the device, but the Home screen holds a lot of surprises!

Explore the Outside of the Kindle Fire

If you're familiar with older Kindle models, you won't see everything you're used to seeing on the outside; that's because the Kindle Fire has a touch screen that enables you to turn pages, make a selection, or access the Home screen without using physical buttons. Because of the touch screen, you don't need much in the way of external controls. All you need is a USB port, a place to plug in headphones, and a power button.

Locate these items on the outside of your Kindle Fire as you hold it upright in portrait view, with the screen facing you:

- **The power button** This is a small, round button located at the bottom of the device. It protrudes a little, making it easy to find by feel alone.

- **The Micro-B connector** This is located to the left of the power button. You use this to connect the power supply and a compatible USB cable (if you want to connect the Kindle Fire to your computer).

- **The headphone input** This small, round, indented input is located to the left of the Micro-B connector. It likely accepts and can use any headphones or ear buds you currently use with other devices.

Explore the Home Screen

When you move the slider to enable your Kindle Fire, you'll see the Home screen. The items that run across the top on the status bar are part of the Kindle Fire's operating system (like the clock and battery icon) and don't change much. This bar also offers notifications when something needs your attention, along with a Wi-Fi indicator and a battery indicator.

CAUTION

If you don't have time to explore your Kindle Fire now, skip toward the end of this chapter and apply a password to your new device before quitting for the day. If you don't, anyone who can access your Kindle Fire can make purchases!

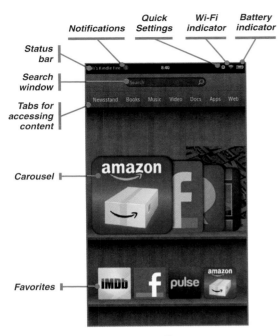

Status bar
Search window
Tabs for accessing content

Notifications | Quick Settings | Wi-Fi indicator | Battery indicator

Carousel

Favorites

Figure 1-2: *The Home screen offers access to everything available on your Kindle Fire.*

TIP

The icons on the Home screen are in a "Carousel." You can flick with a single finger to move quickly through the icons on the Carousel, or you can move through the icons more slowly by leaving your finger on the screen and dragging at whatever speed you like.

What you see in the larger part of the screen will change often, depending on how you've previously used the device. The *Carousel* will show your most recently accessed data, apps, webpages, songs, and the like. You can tap the screen and drag your finger across the icons to browse them. Favorites are underneath this. If you don't see the Home screen shown in Figure 1-2, tap the **Home** icon or the **Back** button shown here. These icons appear when you're away from the Home screen. (If you don't see them, tap the screen once.)

You can tap the first icon in the Carousel to open it. If it's not in the first spot, you can flick through the Carousel entries to place it there. You can also tap any item in the Favorites area to open it. Tapping opens any kind of media on your Kindle Fire. As an example, you can tap an icon for something you've recently accessed, like a book, a webpage, or an app, and the item will open; you can tap a song, and the song will begin to play. If you opt to actually open something though, you'll have to figure out how to close it. It might be best to refrain from this for the moment and simply flick through the Carousel and note what's currently listed in the Favorites area.

There are also tabs that appear just above the Carousel and below the Search window. When you tap one of these, a new screen opens that offers media and data relevant to it. For instance, if you tap the Books option, you gain access to all of the books stored on your Kindle Fire and on Amazon's web servers; if you tap Apps, you'll see the apps that are currently available to you and have access to Amazon's Appstore. You can explore these tabs now, if you like.

To see how the Home screen offers access to what's on your Kindle Fire, work through these steps to familiarize yourself with it:

1. If applicable, tap the **Home** icon to return to the Home screen.
2. Tap the **Quick Settings** icon.
3. Note the available settings shown in Figure 1-3. Tap **Volume**.
4. Move the **Volume** slider left and right to change the volume.

Tap to show a slider that
enables you to change
the screen's brightness

Sync your Kindle Fire
with your cloud content
on Amazon's servers

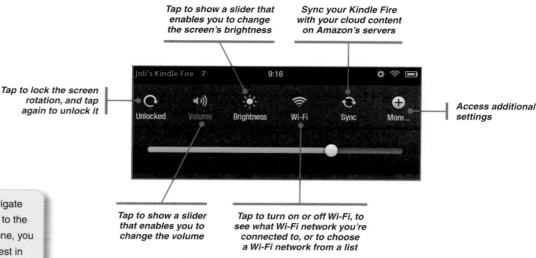

Tap to lock the screen
rotation, and tap
again to unlock it

Access additional
settings

Tap to show a slider
that enables you to
change the volume

Tap to turn on or off Wi-Fi, to
see what Wi-Fi network you're
connected to, or to choose
a Wi-Fi network from a list

*Figure 1-3: **Some settings are "hidden" under the Quick Settings icon.***

 **NOTE**

After you tap an item on the Home screen and navigate away from it, tap the Home or Back icons to return to the Home screen. Depending on how far "in" you've gone, you may have to tap Back more than once. It may be best in many circumstances to simply tap the Home icon.

CAUTION

You must be connected to a Wi-Fi network and the Internet to connect to webpages, the various portions of the Amazon store, and media stored on Amazon's web servers.

5. If you see a number by your name on the status bar (there's a 2 shown in Figure 1-3), tap this number to see the notification. Notifications can be produced by apps to let you know new email has arrived or to offer information about the weather, among other things. Your Kindle Fire can offer notifications about system events as well. Tap anywhere in the status bar to hide it.

6. Tap the **Quick Settings** icon again to hide the additional settings shown in Figure 1-3, or tap either the **Home** or **Back** icon.

7. Tap **Books**. If you've purchased books, you'll see them here, shown in Figure 1-4. If not, tap **Store** to access the Amazon Book store.

8. Tap the **Home** icon to return to the Home screen.

9. Tap **Web**. If small icons appear, they are bookmarks. Tap one to go to the page.

*Figure 1-4: **You may already have some books on your bookshelf.***

LEARNING TAP TECHNIQUES

You know you can tap the icons on the Home screen to access the media they represent. You can do more though. Try the following techniques when exploring a feature that supports it:

- Swipe up and down on the Home screen to see additional entries or to scroll through content at the bottom of a webpage.

- Tap a notification number on the status bar to view notifications.

- Tap the **Quick Settings** icon on the Home screen, and tap and drag to move the slider for brightness and volume.

- Pinch to zoom in and out on content on a webpage.

- Tap and hold an icon to add it to your Favorites or to remove it.

- Tap and hold a URL to display a pop-up window with three choices: Copy, Paste, or Share Page.

- Swipe from left to right to move among pages in a book.

NOTE

If you tap Store on any screen to enter the Book store, Newsstand store, Music store, and so on, *Store* will change to *Library*. You tap Library to return to your own media.

10. Rotate your Kindle Fire 90 degrees left or right to view the page more effectively.

11. Continue to explore as desired.

Explore the Home Screen Tabs

You learned in the previous section how to navigate to and from the available Home screen tabs, namely Books and Web. Although this book will cover in depth how to use the features you'll find under each of these tabs, if you take a few minutes to learn what's available now, you can comfortably explore your Kindle Fire right away. When you're ready to learn more about a particular feature, simply refer to the appropriate chapter in this book.

It's important to understand that most of the tabs on the Home screen, once opened, offer at least two more tabs: Device and Cloud. The Device tab offers access to items stored on your Kindle Fire, and the Cloud tab offers access to what is currently stored on the Internet, on Amazon's servers. (You'll see Store under most of the tabs too, enabling you to easily access related media on Amazon.)

Regarding the Cloud tab: Unless you've specifically placed personal media you own on Amazon's servers, what you see under the Cloud tab will consist of items you've previously purchased from Amazon, and those items will be accessible to view on (or to download to) your Kindle Fire. Because items stored "in the cloud" are stored on Amazon's servers, you will have to be connected to the Internet to access them.

NEWSSTAND

When you tap Newsstand, as with most of the other tabs, you can access both what is on your device and what's stored on Amazon's servers. You won't see any newspapers or magazines under the Device tab unless you've previously subscribed or purchased them. As with other tabs, you can tap Store to access the related Amazon store. The Newsstand store is shown in Figure 1-5. You'll learn about making purchases from the Newsstand store and reading that material in Chapters 2 and 3.

BOOKS

When you tap Books, as with Newsstand, you have access to the Cloud and Device tabs. Store is also available and will take you to the Amazon Book store. If you've purchased Kindle books on other devices, you'll see them under the Cloud tab. To download a book currently stored in the Cloud so that it is available on your Kindle Fire:

1. From the Home screen, tap **Books**.
2. Tap **Cloud**.

*Figure 1-5: **The Newsstand portion of the Amazon store offers magazines and newspapers.***

CAUTION

At the time this book was written, there was no requirement to input a password before making purchases from the Newsstand store, the Book store, the Music store, the Video store, or the Appstore. This means that anyone who can access your Kindle Fire can make purchases from it. Make sure you follow the steps to apply a password to your Kindle Fire as soon as possible, as outlined toward the end of this chapter, to protect your Amazon account.

TIP

To open a book, tap it. Swipe your finger on the screen to move among the pages. To show the controls, tap the screen. Tap the Home icon to return to the Home screen when you're finished reading. You'll learn how to read books in Chapter 3.

NOTE

The functionality detailed here (and for any app discussed in this book) can and will change as Amazon pushes updates to your Kindle Fire.

NOTE

When your free month of Amazon Prime expires, you'll get an email saying so, and you'll have the option to sign up for a year for $79. The trial subscription will not renew automatically.

3. Tap and hold any book you'd like to download, and thus store, on your Kindle Fire.

4. Tap **Download**.

MUSIC

When you tap the Music tab, you gain access to music you've transferred to your Kindle Fire and stored on your device, music that's currently stored in the cloud, and the Amazon MP3 store (Music store). While you may not have any music on your Kindle Fire yet, you may have already made purchases from the MP3 store at Amazon. If that's the case, you will have music available under the Cloud tab.

To see if you have any music on your Kindle Fire or in the cloud:

1. From the Home screen, tap **Music**.

2. Note what appears under the Device tab.

3. Tap **Cloud**.

4. If you find music, tap the new tabs, **Playlists**, **Artists**, **Albums**, and **Songs**, to filter the entries.

5. To learn how to download music to your device, buy music, play music, and perform other tasks, see Chapter 4.

VIDEO

Your new Kindle Fire comes with a full month of Amazon's *Prime* subscription service. Among other things, the subscription includes access to over 10,000 movies and TV shows you can stream to your Kindle Fire, for free, provided you're connected to the Internet. You can access the titles under the Video tab. Your Prime subscription starts the day your device is registered and expires

NOTE

If you do not yet have an account at Amazon.com, create one before you attempt to register your new device. Visit www.amazon.com/myk to get started.

TIP

The Kindle Fire offers you about 6GB of space for storing personal data. That's enough space for 80 apps, plus 10 movies or 800 songs or 6,000 books. Remember though, whatever media you buy from Amazon is stored on Amazon's Internet servers for free, and does not take up any space on your device (unless you specifically request it be downloaded there). You'll learn more about the cloud as you proceed through this book.

30 days after that. Figure 1-6 shows the option to search the Video store for a specific title, as well as some current and popular movies and TV shows. You'll learn all about playing video in Chapter 5.

Figure 1-6: **Prime Instant Videos are free for Prime members.**

APPS

Apps are small programs that can be used to perform calculations, offer information, or enable you to play a game with a friend, among other things. Apps let you listen to audiobooks, check social networking sites, view the local weather forecast, and shop. Some apps come preinstalled on your Kindle Fire. To see them:

1. From the Home screen, tap **Apps**.
2. Tap **Device**.

CAUTION

Before you do anything else, set a password! It's extremely important you password protect your Kindle Fire, because without one (at time this book was written, anyway), anyone who can access your Kindle Fire can buy digital media including apps, music, and even video. Also, make that password hard to guess, and don't write it down inside the pocket of your Kindle Fire case!

NOTE

Write down your password and keep it in a safe place.

You may also have apps stored in the cloud that you've already acquired. To see them, tap **Cloud**. If you want, you can tap and hold any app to download it to your Kindle Fire. You can also tap Store to shop in Amazon's Appstore. The Appstore offers apps that are free and apps you can buy. You'll learn all about Apps in Chapter 6.

Secure and Personalize Your Kindle Fire

There are many ways to personalize your Kindle Fire. You can create a password to secure it, configure various settings for the device and its apps, decide if books and music should be shown in the default grid view or in a list, and more.

Set a Password

Although securing your Kindle Fire with a password should be one of the very first things you do, you really have to know how to move around in the Kindle Fire before you can do it. Although it will take a couple of seconds to access your Kindle Fire when you want to use it, a password will certainly thwart unwanted access by others. It will also keep a thief from accessing your Kindle Fire (and the various Amazon stores, the Appstore, and your personal data), should it fall into the wrong hands. You configure a password under Quick Settings, which you've already explored briefly, so this won't be too difficult a task.

To configure a password for your Kindle Fire:

1. Tap the **Quick Settings** icon on the Home screen.
2. Tap **More**.
3. Tap **Security**. See Figure 1-7.
4. Next to Lock Screen Password, tap **On**.
5. Enter your password in the first box, and reenter it in the second.
6. Tap **Finish**.
7. Tap the **Home** icon.
8. The next time you want access to your Kindle Fire, you'll be prompted to input that new password, as shown in Figure 1-8.

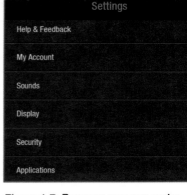

Figure 1-7: *Because you can make purchases from Amazon from your Kindle Fire without typing your password, you should configure a password.*

Figure 1-8: *A password keeps your Kindle Fire safe and secure; make sure you've created a strong one that can't be easily guessed.*

TIP

To test your new password, press the power button to put your Kindle Fire to sleep. Press the power button again, move the slider, input the password, and tap **OK**.

CAUTION

If you make too many changes to how the Kindle Fire looks, what you see in this book and what you see on your device will differ.

Personalize Your Kindle Fire Settings

You can personalize your Kindle Fire by acquiring music, movies, books, magazines, and similar data, and you can also personalize how the Kindle Fire looks and acts when you access that data. For instance, you can set how large the font is when you read a book. You can set how dim or bright you'd like the screen when listening to music, or how loud the music plays. You can configure what search engine Amazon Silk uses too. There are a lot of possibilities. For the most part, there are two ways to access and configure settings: from the Quick Settings icon on the status bar, and from the Menu icon (available on the Options bar) while in an application.

USE THE QUICK SETTINGS ICON

Tap the **Quick Settings** icon on the status bar to gain access to Volume, Brightness, Wi-Fi, and Sync features. You learned earlier from Figure 1-3 that you can tap Volume or Brightness to access the slider and make changes to these settings quickly. You can also access the media controls if you have music

2

3

4

5

6

7

8

9

10

NOTE

While reading a book, the Menu icon offers the option to view the table of contents or sync to the furthest page read on other devices, among other things.

TIP

If your Kindle Fire is lost or stolen, deregister it from the Manage Your Kindle page at any computer connected to the Internet as soon as possible.

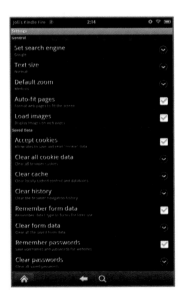

*Figure 1-9: **Many settings are available for the applications on the Kindle Fire; these are a few for Amazon Silk.***

playing or paused; those controls will appear under the Volume or Brightness slider if applicable. Other personalization options are available from the More option that appears, including but not limited to:

- Selecting a new sound theme (Sounds)
- Changing how long the Kindle Fire can be idle before the device sleeps (Display)
- Configuring the keyboard so it produces sounds when you press a key, auto-capitalizes appropriate words, and corrects common typing mistakes (Kindle Keyboard)

To learn how to access these settings and manipulate them, choose a new sound theme now (and note that the steps are similar when making other changes).

1. From the Home screen, tap the **Quick Settings** icon.
2. Tap **More**.
3. Tap **Sounds**.
4. Tap **Notification Sounds**.
5. Tap a new theme.
6. Tap the **Home** icon.

You can see that the options under More are fairly limited. There are quite a few things you'll probably never access, like Legal Notices or Terms of Use, and a few you might access only a little more often, like Sounds and Display. And when you do opt to visit these areas, there's just not that much to configure. Most of the options you'll use often are available from the Menu icon.

USE THE MENU ICON ON THE OPTIONS BAR

Most of the options you'll want access to are available when you're using an app. Figure 1-9 shows only a few of the settings available when you're using the Amazon Silk Web browser. Note that here you can change the search engine, text size, default zoom setting, and more.

NOTE

It's worth noting again that the functionality and options detailed here (and for any app discussed in this book) can and will change as Amazon pushes updates to your Kindle Fire.

NOTE

You can remove some media from your device by tapping and holding the icon on the Home screen. If prompted, tap **Delete** or **Remove From Device**, as applicable. If you opt to remove something from your device that is also stored in the cloud, it will still be available there.

You can also access various settings through the Menu icon. The Menu icon is shown here, and you'll find it in various screens while using your Kindle Fire.

Although you'll learn how to configure settings for each of the applications on the Kindle Fire in their related chapters in this book, take a minute now to locate at least one Menu icon so you can recognize it easily on other screens when it is available. When you tap the Menu icon, you'll be able to see the additional features and settings available for an application.

To access the Menu icon options in Amazon Silk:

1. From the Home screen, tap **Web**.

2. Tap the **Menu** icon on the Options bar.

3. Note the options that appear (see Figure 1-10). You'll learn more about each of these options later, but for now, tap **Settings**.

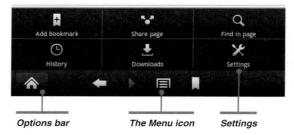

Figure 1-10: *The Menu icon appears at the bottom of quite a few apps, but what you see in each of them differs.*

4. Review the options, but do not make any changes until you've read Chapter 8.

5. Tap the **Home** icon.

Configure Icons on the Home Screen

Finally, you can change how icons appear on the Home screen. To change what appears first in the main area of the Home screen (in the Carousel), tap, hold, and drag your finger across the icons until you come to the one you want to appear first (or want to open). Alternatively, you can use a flicking motion to move more quickly.

QUICKSTEPS

CONNECTING TO A Wi-Fi NETWORK

To locate a Wi-Fi network:

1. Tap the **Quick Settings** icon on the Home screen.

2. Tap **Wi-Fi**.

3. Review the list of networks.

JOIN A SECURE NETWORK

1. From the list of networks, tap the one you want to connect to.

2. Type the password.

3. Tap **Connect**.

JOIN AN OPEN NETWORK

1. From the list of networks, tap the one you want to connect to.

2. Wait while the connection is established.

CAUTION

The Kindle Fire does not currently support any type of pay-as-you-go or subscription service plan for 3G or cellular access. You'll need to seek out and rely solely on free Wi-Fi for Internet access.

NOTE

Once you join a Wi-Fi network, your Kindle Fire will remember it. The next time you're within range of that network, you'll be joined to it automatically.

The icons that appear in the bottom part of the Home screen are Favorites. This list is populated automatically with some default icons when you first get your Kindle Fire, but you can remove what you don't like and add what you do very easily.

To add or remove icons to/from Favorites:

1. In the Carousel, tap and hold (for about a second), any icon you want to add to your Favorites.

2. Tap **Add To Favorites**.

3. Once added to your Favorites, you can tap and hold to access **Remove From Favorites**.

Connect to and Manage Wi-Fi Networks

You may have connected to a password-protected Wi-Fi network when you first turned on your Kindle Fire. You may not have. You may have set up your Kindle Fire at a retail store or a relative's house (and connected to their network), and are now home and want to connect to your own network. Perhaps you'd like to visit your local coffee shop, library, or gym and connect to the unsecured network you know is available there. Whatever the case, there will come a time when you want to connect to a new or different Wi-Fi network.

Locate a Wi-Fi Network

There are generally two areas where you'll find an accessible Wi-Fi network: either in your own home or in a public place like a coffee shop, library, hotel, or pub. Wi-Fi networks are available in homes and businesses and are often protected with a password; those in public places like coffee shops are generally not protected with such.

There are several ways to locate or identify a public Wi-Fi network:

- Ask your friends and family if they know of any free Wi-Fi networks that are close to you.
- From your home computer, perform an Internet search for "Free Wi-Fi Hotspots," followed by your ZIP code.

- Look for signs in the windows of establishments. Most that offer free Wi-Fi say so on a sign that hangs where you can see it.
- Look for an app in the Appstore that will list available Wi-Fi hotspots in your area.
- Turn on your Kindle Fire while in an establishment, and see if a network is detected. Figure 1-11 shows an example of what you might see under Wi-Fi.

Figure 1-11: **To see if networks are available, tap Quick Settings and then tap Wi-Fi.**

Manage Networks

Your Kindle Fire will remember the networks you connect to and will reconnect you automatically each time you get within range. When your Kindle Fire is out of range of a Wi-Fi network, it will continually search until it finds one. It's important to note that the search will start with the list of networks the Kindle Fire has connected to previously.

If you travel regularly and connect to lots of free Wi-Fi networks, the list of networks the Kindle Fire must scan while searching for one can become quite long. A long list takes more time for your Kindle Fire to sift through than a short

UNDERSTANDING THE CLOUD VS. DEVICE STORAGE

The media on your Kindle Fire can be stored and accessed in two places: on the Internet or on your Kindle Fire (or both). When data is stored on the Internet, it's stored "in the cloud." When the data is stored on your Kindle Fire, it's stored "on your device."

THE CLOUD

When you purchase or otherwise obtain media from Amazon, that media is stored for you on Amazon's servers. Although some media is automatically downloaded to your device (like books you buy from the Book store from your Kindle Fire), media such as videos are not. Previous purchases and purchases you make from other devices aren't downloaded to your Kindle Fire automatically either. To be able to access all of the media you've purchased from Amazon, you'll need to be able to access what's stored in the cloud. This is why connecting to a Wi-Fi network is so important. If you aren't connected to the Internet, you can't access the data that is stored there. You can also store your own personal data in the cloud on Amazon's servers. You'll learn more about this in Chapter 4, among other places.

DEVICE

When you opt to store specific media on your Kindle Fire, it's stored on your device. If you know you'll be out of range of Wi-Fi hotspots when you travel with your Kindle Fire, make sure you download the media you want to use on your Kindle Fire before you leave so you'll have access to it.

one, especially if the list contains networks you will likely never connect to again (like one at a hotel or airport). Longer searches require additional battery power too. You should opt to "forget" networks you know you'll never connect to again and "save" ones you know you will.

To save and forget Wi-Fi networks you've previously connected to:

1. Tap the **Quick Settings** icon on the status bar.
2. Tap **Wi-Fi**.
3. Tap and hold the network you want to save or forget and then let go.
4. From the options, tap **Save** or **Forget**. See Figure 1-12. You won't see these options for networks you've never connected to.

*Figure 1-12: **Save networks you access often and forget those you know you'll never connect to again.***

TIP

If you lose the adapter that's required to charge your Kindle Fire using an electrical outlet, use a compatible USB cable to connect it to a computer that's turned on. It'll charge from there.

QUICK**FACTS**

INSTALLING THE KINDLE FIRE APP ON OTHER DEVICES

The books you purchase through your Kindle Fire can often be viewed on other devices. For instance, you can read the books you've purchased from your Kindle Fire on an iPad or an Android phone or tablet, provided you download and install the Kindle Fire app and register the device when prompted. The publishers choose how many devices you access the media on though, and often, the limit is five or six. Amazon places no limits on how many Kindle Fire devices you can register.

Continued . . .

Connect to Your Computer

You don't ever have to connect your Kindle Fire to your computer if you don't want to. The Kindle Fire is unique this way. It can certainly stand alone, provided you have access to a Wi-Fi network to sync and download media like books or music you purchase. If you can't connect your Kindle Fire to the Internet directly though, then you'll have to make your media purchases on your computer and then manually transfer them to your Kindle Fire through the USB cable. (You'll learn how to do this in various chapters in this book.)

Beyond the Wi-Fi issue, though, there are other reasons why you might want to connect your Kindle Fire to your computer: You can transfer personal data easily, including documents, music, and pictures; you can back up what's stored on your Kindle Fire to your computer if you are unsure about the reliability of cloud storage; and you can even charge the device without using the power adapter.

Locate Your Kindle Fire on Your Computer

It's easy to connect the Kindle Fire to the computer; simply connect the smaller end of a Micro-B USB cable to the device and the larger end to the computer's USB port. When you do, the Kindle's screen will inform you that you can now transfer files from your computer to your Kindle Fire, as shown in Figure 1-13. Once connected, you can browse to the Kindle Fire from your computer.

From a Windows-based PC:

1. Click **Start** and click **Computer** (or **My Computer**).
2. Double-click the **Kindle Fire** icon in the Computer window.

INSTALLING THE KINDLE FIRE APP ON OTHER DEVICES *(Continued)*

KINDLE FIRE APP FOR iPAD

On your iPad, visit the Appstore. Search for and download the official Kindle Fire app. When prompted, type your Amazon account name and password, and opt to "register" the device. Once registered, click **Archived** to download any previously purchased book.

KINDLE FIRE APP FOR DROID

On your Droid phone or tablet, visit the Market. Search for and download the official Kindle Fire app. When prompted, type your Amazon account name and password, and opt to "register" the device. Like the iPad, you'll download the previously purchased books as desired.

You can now transfer files from your computer to Kindle.

When you are done, press the disconnect button at the bottom of the screen or eject your Kindle from your computer, and then disconnect the USB cable.

Figure 1-13: **When you see this screen, your Kindle Fire is ready to accept files from your computer.**

3. Note the available folders.

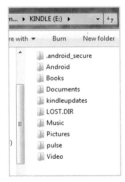

It's best to wait until you know more about your Kindle Fire, including what types of files are compatible, before you transfer any data. However, if you know a little about file types, you can safely transfer songs that are MP3s and pictures that are JPEGs.

4. It is now possible to copy data to the Kindle Fire using any method you prefer. Just make sure to copy data to its respective folder (music to Music, pictures to Pictures). Figure 1-14 shows the Pictures folder on the Kindle Fire open on the left and the Pictures folder on the computer open on the right. It's easy to drag-and-drop pictures when the windows are side by side, as shown here.

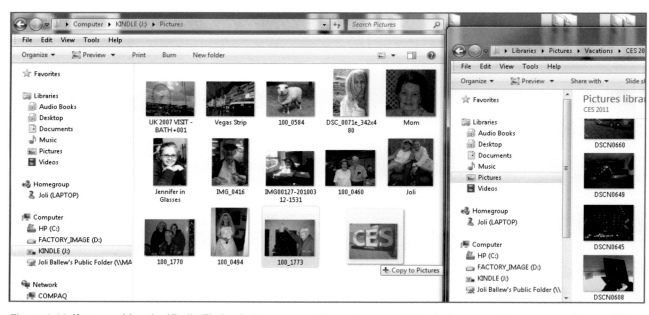

Figure 1-14: If you position the Kindle Fire's window on one side and a computer's window on another, you can drag-and-drop media to copy it.

Chapter 2
Shopping for and Managing Print Content

Your Kindle Fire is perfect for reading books, newspapers, and magazines. It can hold thousands at a time. Books and magazines are easy to navigate, and the Kindle Fire is easy to hold in your hands. This chapter explains how to find the print media you want at the related Amazon stores, get that content on your Kindle Fire, access it, and then manage the content you acquire.

Explore Newsstand and Books

As you learned in Chapter 1, both Newsstand and Books are available options from the Home screen. They offer access to the content stored on your device and what you leave stored in the cloud. Both also offer access to the Amazon store, where you can purchase or obtain additional print media. Figure 2-1 shows Newsstand. Note the two tabs, Cloud and Device, and the option to search the Amazon store for new media.

There are additional options on the Options bar, also shown in Figure 2-1. Home takes you to the Home screen, Back takes you to the previous screen (which may be the Home screen), Menu lets you change the view from Grid to List, and Search lets you search the available content. You'll see the same options under Books.

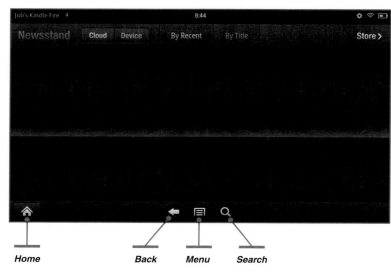

Figure 2-1: *Newsstand offers access to your magazines and newspapers.*

Access and Navigate the Newsstand

The first time you tap Newsstand on the Home screen, you probably won't see any magazines or newspapers there. However, if you replaced an older Kindle model with the new Kindle Fire, you may be able to access the media that you had on the previous device, provided you're using the same Amazon account on both and the media are compatible. If that's the case, you can likely download the previously purchased media to your Kindle Fire. No matter what you see, you'll want to visit the Amazon Newsstand Store and shop around. You can do that from your Kindle Fire if you're connected to a Wi-Fi network.

TIP

If you purchase a magazine or newspaper from Amazon's Newsstand Store from a computer, that content will be downloaded to your Kindle Fire once you're back online with it. The media must be compatible (you'll see notices about this when you make the purchase), but if you shop from the Kindle Newsstand, you shouldn't run into compatibility issues.

ACCESS THE NEWSSTAND STORE FROM THE KINDLE FIRE

Purchasing a magazine or newspaper, obtaining free trials, and downloading content require quite a few steps, so in this section you'll only access and navigate the Newsstand Store. Obtaining and reading Newsstand material gets its own section later in this chapter. That's because while some media is simple to obtain and read using Newsstand (like a single issue of a newspaper), other print media require you to install and download an app first. And when the latter happens, you use that app to access the media *instead of* Newsstand. Don't worry; you'll learn how to do all of that later in the chapter. For now, just access the Newsstand Store from your Kindle Fire.

1. From the Home screen, tap **Newsstand**.

2. Tap **Store**.

3. Scroll left and right and up and down to see what's offered. Figure 2-2 shows some exclusive 90-day free trials.

Figure 2-2: The Newsstand offers free trials of magazines and newspapers.

4. Tap **Search Newsstand Store**.

5. Type something like **Golf**, **Health**, or **Gardening**, or the name of a magazine or newspaper.

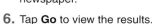

6. Tap **Go** to view the results.

7. Tap **Home**.

ACCESS THE NEWSSTAND FROM A MAC OR PC

If you can't access the Amazon store from your Kindle Fire because it isn't connected to a Wi-Fi network, you can still make purchases from the store using a Mac or a PC (or many other Internet-enabled devices). Those purchases will be transferred to your Kindle Fire the next time you connect to the Internet with it. You can also transfer the data via USB.

To make a newsstand purchase from your computer:

1. Use your web browser to navigate to www.amazon.com.

2. In the left pane, click **Kindle**, and then click **Newsstand**.

3. If you see a magazine or newspaper you like, click its icon to learn more. Later, you'll learn how to buy or subscribe to a magazine.

4. If it's available, click **Available Only On These Devices** to make sure the Kindle Fire is supported before you make a purchase. (You won't always see this option.) Figure 2-3 implies that *Reader's Digest* isn't currently supported (because Kindle Fire isn't listed), but read the Note in the margin for a disclaimer.

NOTE

If you are informed, while shopping at a computer, that a magazine or newspaper isn't Kindle Fire–friendly, that doesn't mean you can't read it on your Kindle Fire. It may be, as is the case with *Reader's Digest,* that you have to download and install the *Reader's Digest* app first. In these cases, it's best to visit a local library or coffee shop, connect to its Wi-Fi, and make the purchase on your Kindle Fire.

Figure 2-3: *When making purchases from a computer, check to see if the magazine or newspaper is supported on the Kindle Fire.*

5. Under the purchasing button in the right pane, select **Kindle Fire** from the list of devices to deliver the content to.

6. On the next page, select your Kindle Fire again and click **Continue**. Your purchase is complete.

Access and Navigate the Book Store

You access and navigate the Book store in the same manner you do with the Newsstand. Tap Books on the Home screen of your Kindle Fire, and you'll be taken to the screen shown in Figure 2-4. Once there, you can view the books on your device or in the cloud, or access the Book store.

Since you may not have any books yet, explore the Amazon Book store first. Just tap Store to enter. Once in the Amazon Book store, it's easy to browse content, and you have access to various categories such as Books, Kindle Singles, Kindle Newsstand, Editors' Picks, Kindle Owners' Lending Library, NY Times Best Sellers, and Children's Picture Books. Figure 2-5 shows these categories. You can also

NOTE

As with newspapers and magazines, you can browse the Amazon Book store from your computer if you can't connect your Kindle Fire to a Wi-Fi network and make purchases and transfer them to your Kindle Fire manually.

CAUTION

At the time this book was written, when you shop for books from your Kindle Fire and tap the price button on any book's Details page, the purchase is complete if you've enabled 1-click. There's no screen that appears to let you "review your purchase" before placing the order. If you're fast enough, you can tap Cancel before the book downloads, although the email notifying you of the refund may take hours to arrive.

Figure 2-4: *The Books tab also offers Cloud, Device, and Store options, like Newsstand.*

Figure 2-5: *From the Book store's "Storefront," tap any category to sort the available content.*

NOTE

You must have an active Amazon Prime subscription to access the Kindle Lending Library. All new Kindle Fire owners are set up with a free, 30-day trial. For more information about Amazon Prime, refer to Chapter 5.

TIP

If you have a local library nearby, visit it and ask how to borrow books and read them on your Kindle. You may be able to borrow several books a month for free.

tap the Menu icon on the Options bar and tap Storefront, Books, Kindle Singles, or Kindle Account. (You'll learn about this later, and this is not shown here.)

To get a feel for how to navigate the Book store on your own:

1. From the Home screen, tap **Books** if applicable.

2. Tap **Store**.

3. Take notice of what's listed under Recommended For You, the Top 100 Paid, and other categories, like Best Fiction of 2012. Scroll up and down and left and right, as applicable.

4. Tap **NY Times Best Sellers**.

5. Scroll up and down to browse the content.

6. Tap any book title to learn more about it.

7. Tap the **Menu** icon and note the options.

8. Tap **Storefront**.

9. Tap the **Menu** icon again; tap **Books**. Note the new view.

10. Tap the **Menu** icon again; tap **Storefront**.

11. Tap **Kindle Owners' Lending Library** and select any category.

12. If you see a book you like and want to borrow it, tap it, and then tap **Borrow For Free**. (You can only borrow one book at a time, and no more than one book a month. You must return the book before you can borrow another.)

13. Tap the **Home** button.

14. Continue exploring as desired.

QUICKSTEPS

SEARCHING FOR SOMETHING SPECIFIC

You may not be able to find what you want by perusing the Book store by category. If you know the book's title or are interested in a particular author, you can use the Search window to type a few keywords. To search for something specific in the Book store:

1. In the Book store, tap **Search Book Store**.

2. Type a few keywords.

3. Tap **Go**.

4. Note the results and tap one to see the book's Details page.

Borrow Public Library Books

You can borrow Kindle books from more than 11,000 libraries in the United States. You can read those books on your Kindle Fire, among other places. You'll need to do a little research of your own to get started, though. For instance, the library you want to borrow from must offer online services that support lending to your Kindle Fire; a simple call to your local library will provide this information. You'll also need a library card from that library.

Here's a summary of what you'll need to do before you can borrow and read books on your Kindle Fire:

1. Navigate to the website of a U.S. library that offers Kindle Fire lending support.

2. Check out a Kindle book (library card required).

3. Click **Get For Kindle**.

4. You'll be directed to Amazon.com, and you'll likely need to log in there. Wait for the download to complete.

Explore Categories, Read Reviews, and More

When you tap a category while shopping in the Amazon Book store, the results are shown by what is the most popular (bestselling). However, you may want to search the results by publication date, by price, or by average customer review. You may also want to learn more about a book before you buy it, read customer reviews, see a book's sales rank, or even see the file size, among other things.

SORT BOOKS IN A CATEGORY

When you tap a category, like Editors' Picks, the books are listed in a particular order. Specifically, books are sorted by Bestselling. To sort the items in another way:

1. In the Book store, tap the **Menu** icon and tap **Storefront**.

2. Tap **Editors' Picks**.

3. Tap **Refine**.

NOTE

You'll learn how to write your own review in Chapter 3.

Figure 2-6: *In the Storefront, when you tap Books, you are prompted to choose a category to sort the results.*

4. Tap the **Sort By: Bestselling** arrow.

5. Tap another choice to sort the books.

Back at the Storefront, note that Books is another option. When you tap Books, you aren't taken to another page. Instead, you are prompted to choose a category, as shown in Figure 2-6. Another option from the Storefront, the Kindle Owners' Lending Library, also offers the option to sort by category.

READ EDITORIAL REVIEWS

People will sometimes write reviews of books they have read, and the reviews may help you decide if you want to purchase a book or not. While many readers' reviews focus on the content of the book, others may focus on how the book appears on the Kindle Fire.

To locate and read reviews for a book (and to see what customers also bought):

1. Using any navigation method, locate a book you're considering purchasing.

2. Tap the book's icon to access the Details page.

3. From the Details page, scroll down to the reviews. See Figure 2-7.

4. As always, tap the **Home** icon to return to the Home screen, or tap the **Back** icon to return to the previous screen.

Figure 2-7: *If reviews are available, they'll be near the bottom of the Details page.*

Buy and Download Print Content

Once you've navigated to a book or newspaper that you want, it's easy to obtain it. In fact, some may say it's a little too easy if you enabled 1-click when first prompted to; you simply tap the icon that shows the price of the item and it's yours! There's no page that asks you to confirm your purchase, and you don't have to input a password. Thus, you should be very sure you want to buy an item before tapping the price button.

It's not quite as easy to obtain magazines, because as you learned earlier, some magazines require you download an app first. Once the app is installed, you can then download and read the publication.

Download a Free Book

To minimize unintended purchases, in this section you'll learn how to get a free e-book first, and then later you can opt to make purchases. The process is the same, only here your credit card won't be charged!

From your Kindle Fire's Home screen:

1. Tap **Books**, and then tap **Store**.
2. Tap inside the Search window, and then type **free books for kindle**.
3. Tap **Refine** to change the order of the list and/or scroll through the list to locate a book you'd like to download.
4. Tap **Free** when you've found a book you like.

5. On the book's Details page, tap **Buy For Free**.

6. After the book downloads, tap **Read Now**.

7. To exit the book and return to the Home screen, tap the screen once and tap the **Home** button.

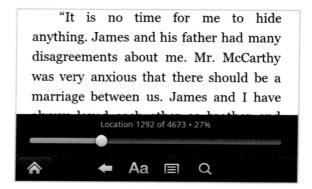

> "It is no time for me to hide anything. James and his father had many disagreements about me. Mr. McCarthy was very anxious that there should be a marriage between us. James and I have

Location 1292 of 4673 • 27%

Get a Free Trial of a Magazine

You learned earlier how to browse the Newsstand store for magazines, but you may not know that it's fairly easy to try a magazine for free through a trial subscription. If you decide you like the magazine, do nothing, and you'll be billed when the trial is over. After that the magazine will be automatically delivered to your Kindle Fire each month. If you don't like the magazine or don't want to pay for a yearly subscription, simply cancel the membership within the trial period and you won't be billed.

During the process of selecting and downloading a magazine, you may be prompted to download an app to go along with it. For example, both *Wired* and *Reader's Digest* require their own apps, and once installed, you must use the app to read the publication. (See Chapter 3 for more information about this and Chapter 6 for more information about apps in general.) Other magazines won't require you to install an app. *Shape,* for instance, can be downloaded directly to the Newsstand and read there.

NOTE

The free trial period for a magazine can differ. Some free trials will offer 90 days, while others will only offer 14.

NOTE

If you opt for a free trial of a specific magazine, say Shape, and then cancel it, you can't go back at a later time and get another free trial for that same magazine. You can, however, have multiple free trials at the same time, perhaps one for *Shape*, one for *Reader's Digest*, and one for *Wired*.

NOTE

To cancel a trial subscription (and this is more easily achieved at a computer), navigate to Amazon.com, go to your account, and then select **Manage Your Kindle**. Click **Magazines**. Under Actions, for the magazine you want to cancel, click **Cancel Subscription**.

To get a free trial to a magazine of your choice, from your Kindle Fire:

1. From the Home screen, tap **Newsstand**.
2. Tap **Store**.
3. Look around for free trial offers. Earlier in Figure 2-2 you saw several magazines that were available for a 90-day free trial. Most magazines though only offer a 14-day trial period.
4. Once you find a magazine you'd like to try, tap its icon.
5. Read the information offered about the price. It's likely you'll see the options shown in Figure 2-8. Notice if you tap **Subscribe Now**, you'll be automatically enrolled in the free trial.

Figure 2-8: All magazines offer a free trial if you select Subscribe Now.

6. If you are prompted to download an app, you'll have to work through the resulting screens to do so; tap **Download** to obtain the media when the process is complete.
7. Refer to Chapter 3 to learn how to read a magazine or book. For now, remember to cancel the subscription within the trial window if you don't want to be billed.

NOTE

Chapter 3 covers how to read books on your Kindle Fire.

As you acquire and read magazines, you'll notice that back issues are grouped to help you keep your Newsstand organized. In addition, your Kindle Fire will automatically delete issues that are more than seven issues old. This keeps your Kindle Fire from filling up with old content. If you want to keep an issue, press and hold it and select Keep. You can also add it to your Favorites, where it will be kept on your Kindle until you delete it.

Buy Books and Newspapers

TIP

If you find that you want to download media but don't have enough space on your Kindle to hold it, you will need to delete some data first. This is covered later in the chapter.

You already know how to buy a book. It's the same process as obtaining a free book. You locate the book, tap the price button, and the book will download. Newspapers in the Newsstand store are the same. If you're purchasing from

a computer, the book will be delivered the next time your Kindle connects to the Internet via Wi-Fi and you opt to sync it, or when you connect your Kindle and opt to transfer the media manually.

For the sake of completeness, here's how to buy a book from Amazon's Book store, from your Kindle Fire:

1. Tap **Books** on the Home screen.
2. Browse to the book you'd like to buy.
3. Tap the book's icon.
4. Tap the price of the book.
5. Wait while the book downloads automatically.

Manually Download Content

If you have a situation where you make purchases from a computer or other tablet (like an iPad, another Kindle, or a Motorola Xoom) and want to access that content on your Kindle Fire, you'll need to manually download it. You can access purchased media under the Cloud tab of either Newsstand or Books, and from there, perform the download to your Kindle Fire.

To manually download a book you purchased from the Amazon Book store to your Kindle Fire:

1. Tap **Books** from the Home screen.
2. Tap the **Cloud** tab.
3. Locate the purchase, and tap and hold its icon for one second.
4. Tap **Download**.

Access and Manage Content

Now that you've made a purchase or two, you need to know where that content is stored on your Kindle Fire and how to access it. Books from Amazon are under the Books tab (books you get from other sources may appear under Docs), newspapers appear under the Newsstand tab, and magazines will either appear under Newsstand or under a related app. With that done, you need to know how to manage content—specifically, how to remove media you no longer want access to from your Kindle Fire and how to add your favorites to the Favorites area.

Access Content

You understand that some content is stored on your Kindle Fire and some is stored in the cloud. When you're connected to a Wi-Fi network, you can access either. When you're not connected to a Wi-Fi network, you'll only be able to access data you've specifically downloaded to your device or copied to it from a computer.

To access books you've obtained:

1. From the Home screen, tap **Books**.
2. Tap **Cloud** to see books you own and to download them to your Kindle Fire.
3. Tap **Device** to see books you have on your Kindle Fire.
4. If you know you have more content than what's shown, flick up and down on the screen.
5. To open a book, tap it one time. You'll learn how to read media in Chapter 3.
6. To close a book, tap the screen one time and tap the **Home** icon.

To access a newspaper:

1. From the Home screen, tap **Newsstand**.
2. Tap **Cloud** to see newspapers you have access to.
3. Tap **Device** to see newspapers stored on your Kindle Fire.
4. If you know you have more content than what's shown, flick up and down on the screen.
5. To open a newspaper, tap it one time. You'll learn how to read media in Chapter 3.
6. To close a newspaper, tap the screen one time and tap the **Home** icon.

NOTE

The functionality detailed here (and for any app discussed in this book) can and will change as Amazon pushes updates to your Kindle Fire.

NOTE

You might think that, like other tablet computers, you could organize content on your Kindle Fire into groups or folders. Perhaps you'd like to create a folder under the Books tab and name it Travel, and drag all of the books you own that involve travel to it. You can't do that yet, but it's likely you'll be able to in the future. This is worth mentioning, because by the time you get this book, those features may indeed be available. To find out, tap and hold any item under Newsstand or Books and see if there are any additional options.

To access a magazine from Newsstand:

1. From the Home screen, tap **Newsstand.**
2. Tap **Cloud** to see magazines you own.
3. Tap **Device** to see magazines you have on your Kindle Fire.
4. If you know you have more content than what you can see, flick up and down on the screen. If you don't see the magazine, or you remember downloading an app at the same time you acquired the periodical, skip to the next procedure.
5. To open a magazine, tap it one time. You'll learn how to read media in Chapter 3.
6. To close a magazine, tap the screen one time and tap the **Home** icon.

To access a magazine that requires an app:

1. From the Home screen, tap **Apps**.
2. Tap **Device**.
3. Locate the app that represents the magazine and tap it to open. Figure 2-9 shows two magazine apps: one is for *Reader's Digest* and the other for *Wired Magazine.*
4. Tap **View**.
5. To close the magazine and the app, tap the screen one time to view the controls.
6. Tap the **Home** icon. In apps, it's often at the top of the screen instead of the bottom. If you tap a Home icon at the top of a page, you will also have to tap the Home icon that appears at the bottom to get to the Home screen.

Figure 2-9: Some magazines require you to read them using an app.

Readers Digest November 2011

Organize Content

There isn't much you can do yet with regard to organizing the print content you keep on your Kindle Fire. You can't create folders and move data into them or rearrange items on the screen, for instance. About all you can do is delete content you no longer want on the device, keep a specific periodical on your Kindle Fire even after a new issue comes out, and add print content to Favorites. To access the options, tap and hold the print media's icon. Figure 2-10 shows the options available for a single newspaper edition from the Home screen. One of those options is Remove From Device. Use this often; in fact, it's best to delete media you've read every other month or so. This helps keep your Kindle Fire from getting full, but it also makes it easier to find what you want. If you only keep data on the Kindle Fire you want to access, what's there will always be relevant to you.

Figure 2-10: *Tap and hold the icon for any print content to see the options.*

Buy and Transfer Content Using a Computer

There are two reasons why you'd want to transfer print media from your computer to your Kindle Fire using a computer and a USB cable. Either there's no Wi-Fi available for your Kindle Fire for making purchases and downloading Amazon content or you have print media on your computer that you did not purchase from Amazon that you want to copy to it. The latter may be the case if you obtained free books from third parties (including libraries) and that content could not be sent directly to your device. Whatever the scenario, before you can transfer media from your computer to your Kindle Fire, the media must be downloaded to your computer or currently stored on it.

Purchase Digital Items on a Computer

Data that is stored on your computer can be copied to your Kindle Fire. This means that any digital purchases you make at Amazon.com from your computer must be downloaded to your computer before you can transfer the data to your Kindle Fire. The same is true from other websites; you must download what you purchase before you can even think about transferring it to your Kindle Fire via USB. When making digital purchases, make sure you select the option to transfer via computer, download, or save when making the purchase. (If this isn't an option, as with newspapers and most magazines, you're out of luck.)

To make purchases from Amazon and to set those purchases up for manual transfer to your Kindle Fire (making purchases from other websites is similar):

1. From your computer, at Amazon.com, locate the item you want to purchase.

2. Choose **Transfer via Computer**. If you don't see this option, you can't obtain and transfer the media in this manner.

3. Opt to make the purchase using Buy Now With 1-Click or another option.

4. In the Deliver To box that appears, select your Kindle Fire and click **Continue**.

5. When prompted, click **Save**.

6. When the download completes, click **Open Folder**.

7. Leave this window open. Continue to the next section to connect your Kindle Fire to your computer and copy this file to it.

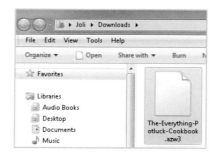

UNDERSTANDING WHY SHOPPING FROM A COMPUTER IS OFTEN EASIER

It's generally best to shop for digital content from your Kindle Fire when you can. What you buy is immediately available, and there's no need to connect to a computer and manually transfer your media later. However, there are reasons why you might prefer to shop from a computer, and if that's the case, certainly do so. For example:

- A computer offers a larger screen and the books, reviews, and author pages are easier to see.
- You can use a mouse, making the Amazon store easier to navigate.
- You have easy access to your Amazon Account, Manage Your Kindle, and Kindle Support webpages.
- You can better see images of Kindle accessories, including cases, covers, sleeves, and power adapters.

CAUTION

Make sure you copy the files instead of moving them. When you copy files, the original remains on your computer and a copy is placed on your Kindle. This enables you to keep a backup of the files on your computer and continue to access them there.

Transfer Digital Content to Your Kindle Fire

To transfer downloaded data to your Kindle Fire, connect it via the USB cable as outlined in Chapter 1. Then browse to the desired folder on the Kindle Fire that you want to transfer media to. Put Books in the Books folder, for instance. If you put a book in the Books folder but can't access it later, connect it again and put it in the Documents folder. It may transfer successfully then, depending on what it is, and become accessible there.

To copy compatible books from your computer to your Kindle:

1. Connect your Kindle using the available USB cable.
2. On a PC:
   a. Click **Start**.
   b. Click **My Computer** (or **Computer**).
   c. Double-click your Kindle in the resulting window.
3. On a Mac:
   a. Open **Finder**.
   b. Click your Kindle in the left pane under Devices.
4. Position this window to take up half of the screen.
5. Open a similar window and browse to the location of the book(s) or files(s) you want to copy. Position this window to take up approximately half the screen. See Figure 2-11.
6. Using any method you're familiar with, copy the desired files to the Documents folder on the Kindle. Dragging-and-dropping is a common way to transfer files.
7. Wait until all of the files are copied, and then disconnect your Kindle.

If you want to drag-and-drop files from sources other than Amazon, make sure they are of a compatible file format. If they aren't, even though they will copy, you won't be able to open them. The compatible formats for documents include Kindle (.azw), text (.txt), and Mobi (.mobi*, .prc*, and .doc). You can find out the format of a file by right-clicking it, selecting **Properties**, and choosing the **Details** tab on a PC (Macs offer similar information). See Figure 2-12.

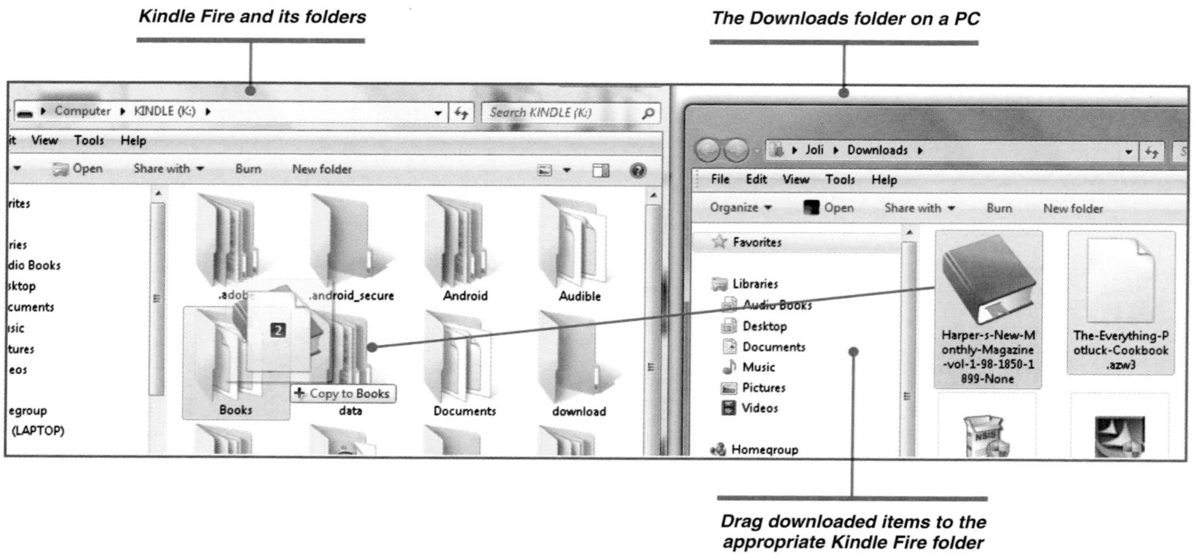

Kindle Fire and its folders

The Downloads folder on a PC

**Drag downloaded items to the
appropriate Kindle Fire folder**

Figure 2-11: Drag downloaded media to the appropriate folder on the Kindle Fire.

CAUTION

Files containing digital rights management software will
not be readable.

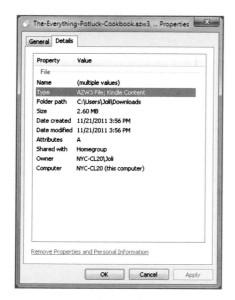

*Figure 2-12: The Properties page for a file
shows its file format.*

How to...

Chapter 3
Reading Newspapers, Magazines, and Books

You learned in Chapter 2 how to get print content on your Kindle Fire and how to manage it. You also learned where to locate the content you've acquired, using Books, Newsstand, and Apps. In this chapter, you'll learn how to read and browse the print media you've obtained, and how to create bookmarks, change reading options, make notes, and look up the meanings of words, among other things. Once you're familiar with how to read content on your Kindle Fire, you'll learn a little about how to access your books from your computer and other mobile devices.

Read Newspapers and Magazines

If you acquired a newspaper or a magazine in Chapter 2, you're probably anxious to read it! There are only a few steps: find the content, open it, and browse through it. Figure 3-1 shows sample Newsstand content. If you don't see the magazine you're looking for here, you'll have to look under the Apps tab. As you learned in the previous chapter, some magazines come with their own app and must be read using that app. Newspapers will always appear under the Newsstand tab.

Figure 3-1: *Newsstand content can include newspapers and magazines.*

Read a Magazine

If you have a lot of content, either under Newsstand or under Apps, swipe your finger left and right or up and down until you find the item you'd like to read. Once you've found something, tap it once to open it. (You may also be able to access recent items from the Home screen.) Figure 3-2 shows the cover of the November 2011 issue of *National Geographic,* along with the controls that appear when you tap the screen.

The controls you have access to while reading a magazine will differ depending on how you're reading it. If you're reading it in Newsstand, the controls appear as shown in Figure 3-2; if you're reading it from inside an interactive app, the controls will appear in other places, and will offer both similar and different

CAUTION

Unless Amazon has pushed out a security update, anyone who can gain access to your Kindle Fire can buy print content using your Amazon account and your Kindle Fire. If you haven't taken steps to protect your Kindle Fire with a password, return to Chapter 1 now to learn how.

TIP

The controls that appear when you tap a magazine include a slider that you can use to navigate through the pages in the magazine quickly.

3

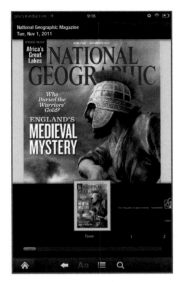

QUICKSTEPS

READING A MAGAZINE IN TEXT VIEW

By default, a magazine that is opened in Newsstand will be offered to you in "Page" view. In this view, the pages on the screen look exactly like what you see in the printed publication. If the print appears too small or if you're constantly zooming in or out, you can switch to "Text" view. Text view may be easier to read for other reasons, too, since it appears on the screen more like a book than a magazine.

To switch from Page view to Text view:

1. With a magazine open, browse to a page that does not have a full-page advertisement.

2. Tap the **Menu** icon on the Options bar.

3. Tap **Text View**. It will turn orange once selected.

| Page View | Text View |

4. Tap the **Menu** icon to hide these controls.

5. Flick through the pages as usual. Tap the screen to view additional controls, which include left and right arrows for navigation.

Figure 3-2: A digital magazine will look very much like a printed one, complete with color pictures and identical page layouts.

functionalities. If all you want to do is read the magazine from start to finish, flicking may be enough. If not, read on to learn how to use the other options.

READ A MAGAZINE IN NEWSSTAND

With a magazine open from Newsstand:

- Use a finger to "flick" through the pages by swiping left and right.
- Tap to access the controls.
- With the controls available, use the slider to move through the pages in the magazine, and then tap the thumbnail of any page to view it. See Figure 3-3.
- To hide the controls, tap the page on the screen.
- Pinch outward to zoom in or out of page content.
- Tap on the left or right margin to move among pages.
- If a hyperlink is available, you can click it to open Amazon Silk and go to the page.
- To close the magazine, tap the screen and tap the Home icon.

Thumbnails

Page numbers

Slider

Figure 3-3: When you move the slider, thumbnails of the pages appear; tap one to read that page.

READ A MAGAZINE IN AN INTERACTIVE APP

If the magazine isn't available in the Newsstand, you'll find it under Apps. When you click the app associated with a magazine under the Apps tab, you have the option to *archive* the issue or *view* it. Tap **View** to open it. Then, with a magazine open from an app:

- Use a finger to "flick" through the pages by swiping left and right.

- Tap to access the controls. If you tap an ad, you may see an option to buy the product. Likewise, if you tap a hyperlink, you'll be taken to the associated webpage.

- With the controls available, use the slider to move through the pages in the magazine. Let go to stop at the selected page to view it.

- To hide the controls, tap the page on the screen, or wait for the controls to disappear on their own.

- If you see a down arrow, flick to see more content.

> elderly man
> alker. When
> d seen only
> cks, pointed
> n 1959!"

To close a magazine you're viewing in an app:

1. Tap the screen one time to show the controls.

2. Tap the **Home** icon at the top of the page.

3. In the resulting page, tap the **Home** icon again. (If you're finished with the magazine, you can tap **Archive**.)

There are a handful of other app-related features to explore. For instance, when you tap to show the controls, you'll see additional options across the top of the app. In Figure 3-4, the lined icon offers access to various parts of this issue, including the cover, instructions for using the app, the table of contents, and more. You can also see the Back and Home icons here.

Figure 3-4: Apps contain their own set of controls, which can differ from app to app.

If you tap the lined icon on the right (shown in Figure 3-4), a new view appears, with the articles appearing in vertical lines. Here you can see how this looks for a *Reader's Digest* publication. Tap the icon again to leave this view.

Change Reading Options for Newspapers and Magazines

After you've read for a bit, you may want to change the reading options. At the present time, magazines in apps don't allow you to change the font, typeface, or margin size because if you could change these features, the layout of the magazine would be disrupted. Pages would not appear as they do in the actual publications.

However, you can change the font style, line spacing, margins, and color mode of magazines you read in the Newsstand (among other things), provided you opt to view the magazine in Text view first.

To change the reading options for magazines in Newsstand:

1. Open the magazine.
2. Tap the screen and tap the **Menu** icon.
3. Tap **Text View**.
4. Tap the **Menu** icon again.
5. Tap the screen and tap the **Text** icon. It's the icon with "Aa" on it. See Figure 3-5.

Figure 3-5: *In Text view, options are available to change the font style, color mode, and more.*

6. To make a change, simply tap the desired item.
7. Tap the page or the **Menu** icon again to hide the options.

TIP

To exit a magazine in Newsstand, tap the screen and tap the Home icon.

QUICKSTEPS

READING NEWSPAPERS

Reading a newspaper is a little different from reading a magazine. First, newspapers aren't generally laid out the same way magazines are, where the page looks the same on the Kindle Fire's screen as it does in the magazine. If newspapers were laid out this way, the text would be too small to read. In addition, newspaper content is organized into sections (Front Page, Business, Sports, etc.), and those sections contain articles. Thus, reading newspapers on the Kindle Fire requires you to first select the newspaper section you want to read, and then tap an article in that section to read it. Once you have an article on the screen, you flick to view content.

To read a newspaper in Newsstand:

1. From the Home screen, tap **Newsstand** and tap a newspaper to read.

2. Tap **Sections**, and then tap a section of the paper to read.

3. Flick through the content and tap any article to read it.

4. Scroll left and right to read the content.

5. Tap the screen to view the controls, which are similar to the magazine controls you've already explored.

6. Tap the **Menu** icon to leave the current article and choose another section of the paper, or to access the Home icon.

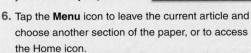

Work Crosswords, Read Comics, and Learn More

At the time this book was written, there wasn't too much available that allowed you to interact with newspapers and magazines. Specifically, there was no crossword or word jumble to work in *USA Today,* no videos to play in *The Onion,* and very few comics to read in any of the available newspapers. As time passes, you can be sure these features will become available, though. In fact, it may be that by the time you get this book, you'll be able to do all of those things! That said, it's important to note that when these features do become available, you should feel safe accessing and using them. It's nearly impossible to damage your Kindle Fire by tapping the wrong thing or tapping an available screen element.

Read Books

Your books are available under the Books tab on the Home screen. As you learned in Chapter 2, books you've downloaded to your device are available from the Device tab located there. Figure 3-6 shows an example. To open a book under the Device tab, simply tap it.

The Cloud tab offers access to all of the books you've obtained from Amazon. If the book has a down arrow on it, it's available for download. If it does not have an arrow, it's already been downloaded to your Kindle Fire. If you like, you can open and read a book you've already downloaded from under this tab as well as from the Device tab.

With a book open, there are several ways to move among the pages, but the most popular are the following:

- Tap in the left or right margin to move to the previous page or the next page, respectively.
- Flick left and right to move to the previous page or the next page, respectively.
- Tap once to show the controls, and drag the slider left or right to move through a book quickly.

Figure 3-6: Books listed under the Books
Device tab are ready for reading.

As you read, you can keep up with your progress using the timeline at the
bottom of the page. Just tap the page to see it. When you do, you'll also see
familiar icons: Home, Back, Text, Menu, and Search. Figure 3-7 shows these
controls.

Figure 3-7: Tap toward the middle of any book's page
to access these options.

Each icon has a specific function:

- Tap **Home** to close the book and return to the Home screen.
- Tap **Back** to go back to the previous screen or page.
- Tap **Text** to change the font style, typeface, line space, margins, and color mode.

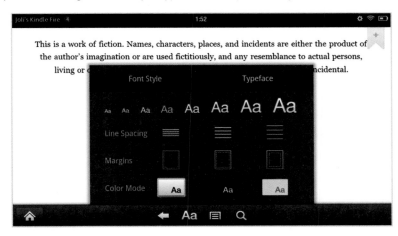

- Tap **Menu** to move to a different area of the book, such as the cover or table of contents, to see notes and marks, and more.
- Tap **Search** to type a word to find in the book.

Set Reading Preferences for Books

After reading a book for a while, you may decide you need to make a few changes to how the text appears on the screen. You may also decide you'd like to lock the screen rotation so that it doesn't inadvertently change while you're handling your Kindle Fire.

To access reading preferences options and make changes:

1. While reading a book, tap the screen to show the options.
2. Tap the **Text** icon.
3. Tap the desired choices under the Font Style options, including the font size, line spacing, margins, and color mode.

TIP

If you have poor eyesight, choose a larger font and set Line Spacing to the largest setting possible. You may also prefer white text on a black background, one of the options from the Text icon on the Options bar.

CHANGING THE TYPEFACE

Some fonts are easier on the eyes than others. You can choose a new font from the Text options.

1. While reading a book, tap the screen to show the options.

2. Tap **Typeface**.

3. Tap a new font from the list. The list is scrollable, and additional fonts are available under what's shown.

4. Tap the **Text** icon again to hide the options.

4. Tap the **Text** icon to hide it.

5. To lock the screen so that it won't change from portrait to landscape view (or vice versa), tap the **Quick Settings** icon on the status bar (not shown). Tap **Unlocked** (it will change to Locked).

Find the Table of Contents, Beginning, Page Locations, and More

If you're reading a novel, you probably won't need to skip to a particular page, access the table of contents, or even search for a word. If you're reading something else, however, like a study guide, textbook, the Bible, or a similar reference, you'll probably need to access specific pages or places quite often. You can move to a particular place in a book from the Menu icon.

1. While reading a book, tap the screen.

2. Tap the **Menu** icon on the Options bar.

3. Tap any option, shown in Figure 3-8.

Figure 3-8: *Tap to access a particular place in a book, or to name your own location (often a page number).*

For the most part, the options are self-explanatory.

- **Cover**   Accesses the book's front cover.
- **Table of Contents**   Accesses the first page of the table of contents.
- **Beginning**   Accesses the first page of the book.
- **Location**   Use this to type in your own specific place in a book. For this option, it's important to note that the page numbers you see on your Kindle Fire won't match the page numbers in the actual book.
- **Sync to Furthest Page**   Accesses the furthest page in the book that you've read across all compatible devices. For instance, if you read on an iPad as well as the Kindle Fire, and you recently read a chapter on the iPad, you can skip to that point on your Kindle Fire using this option.
- **My Notes & Marks**   Use this to view and access your notes and marks. You may not have any, as Figure 3-8 shows.

Create and Access Bookmarks

Bookmarks on your Kindle Fire are like bookmarks you create in a book. They are reference points you can return to when they're needed. There's no need to create a bookmark to save your place as you would in a physical book, though; your Kindle Fire will remember where you left off the next time you open it. Instead, you'll create bookmarks because you want to return to that point in the book later and reference it for one reason or another. You may want to bookmark the moment the butler walks into the room in a whodunit, your favorite passage in a book, or the first use of a specific word, for instance. Once you've created a bookmark, you can easily return to it by taping the Menu button and choosing View Notes & Marks.

To create a bookmark:

1. While in a book, tap the screen to show the controls.
2. Tap the bookmark icon in the upper-right corner. It will turn blue once set.

USING THE DICTIONARY

If you come across a word you don't know the meaning of, you can look it up.

1. Tap the word and hold for about a second.

2. Note the definition that appears.

3. If desired, tap **Full Definition**.

4. If you opt to view the full definition, tap the screen and tap the **Back** icon to return to the book.

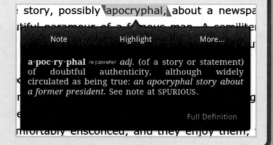

NOTE

Most of the time, you can tap outside any options window to hide it.

To access a bookmark you've created:

1. Tap the screen to show the controls and tap the **Menu** icon.

2. Note the View Notes & Marks section.

3. Tap any bookmark to go to that page.

4. To return to the previous place in the book, tap the screen and tap the **Back** icon.

Use Book Controls and Features

You've explored some of the available book settings, including how to change the font size and line spacing, and a few features, such as how to navigate to a specific page in a book, among other things. There is quite a bit more to explore though.

Make Notes, Highlight Text, and Use Search

You can make notes about a specific word or passage in a book and highlight words and passages, and then access those notes and marks from the Menu option. Notes are especially useful when added to study materials, and highlights can be helpful in keeping up with shady characters, possible weapons, and motives in mystery novels. You can also search for a word or phrase in a book, or on Wikipedia or Google, if you'd like more information about it. Figure 3-9 shows the options for Note and Highlight, and the search options are available under More.

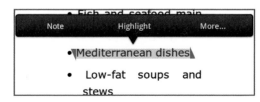

Figure 3-9: Tap and hold any text, and these options will appear.

MAKE A NOTE

A note is text you write about a word, passage, paragraph, page, or chapter. To start a note, you simply tap and hold a word on the page. When the option to create a note appears, you can drag from the edges of the blue handles to choose what text to call out for the note.

To create a note:

1. While in a book, tap the screen for a second. Lift up when you see blue highlighting underneath, which should take less than a second.
2. Drag from the blue handles to choose the text to apply the note to. Figure 3-9 shows an example.
3. Tap **Note**.
4. Type your note and tap **Save** when finished.

HIGHLIGHT TEXT

Highlighting is another way to call out text so that you can reference it later. To highlight text:

1. While in a book, tap the screen for a second. Lift up when you see blue highlighting underneath, which should take less than a second.
2. Drag from the blue handles to choose the text to apply the highlight to.
3. Tap **Highlight**.

SEARCH FOR A WORD OR PHRASE

To search for a word or a phrase in a book or on the Internet:

1. While in a book, tap the screen for a second. Lift up when you see blue highlighting underneath, which should take less than a second.
2. Drag from the blue handles to choose the text to search for.
3. Tap **More**.
4. Tap **Search In Book**, **Search Wikipedia**, or **Search Google**. The last two options may not be available if you are searching anything more than a word or two. See Figure 3-10.
5. Tap the **Back** icon to return to your place in the book.

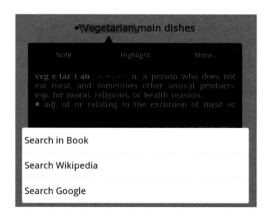

Figure 3-10: **When searching for words, all three of the Search options will be available.**

Read Kindle Books on a Computer

You learned in Chapter 1 that you can install the Kindle app on mobile devices and read your Kindle books there. These devices include iPads, various Android-based phones, BlackBerry phones, Windows 7 phones, and more. You can also read your Kindle books on a Windows-based PC or an Apple Mac. You may have already explored some of this and installed an app on one of your devices to test it. You probably have not explored the art of reading books on your computer though. There are two ways to do this. You can download and install the Kindle app for your computer, or you can use the Cloud Reader.

Explore the Kindle App on a PC or Mac

There is a Kindle application available for your PC or your Mac. It's a program, and must be downloaded and installed like any other computer program. You can find it for your Windows computer at www.amazon.com/KindleForPC and for your Mac at the Apple Store. Figure 3-11 shows what the application looks like once installed and opened on a PC.

The first time you use the Kindle app, shown in Figure 3-12, you'll be instructed on how to use your computer mouse or trackpad to move among the pages. You'll also see familiar menus like File, View, and Tools, among others, that offer features you'd expect to see. For instance, from the View menu, you can opt to view the book in full-screen mode, show your notes and marks, and change the color mode.

Here are a few of the features you'll have access to (this is not a complete list):

- You can access your Kindle books from your computer and incorporate full-screen reading.
- The application synchronizes the last page you read on either your computer or your device so that no matter what device you are using, you can always start reading where you left off.
- You can use the dictionary; create notes, highlights, and bookmarks; and use a search feature.

CAUTION

Kindle newspapers, magazines, and blogs are not currently available for Kindle for PC or Kindle for Mac.

NOTE

When you make a purchase on any Internet-enabled device from the Kindle store, that purchase registers with Amazon. This means you can download that item to any compatible device later, including your Kindle Fire.

CAUTION

By the time you purchase this book, it might be that more web browsers and devices are supported. Before you download Chrome or Safari, or upgrade your operating system, try to access the Cloud Reader using your desired device and configuration.

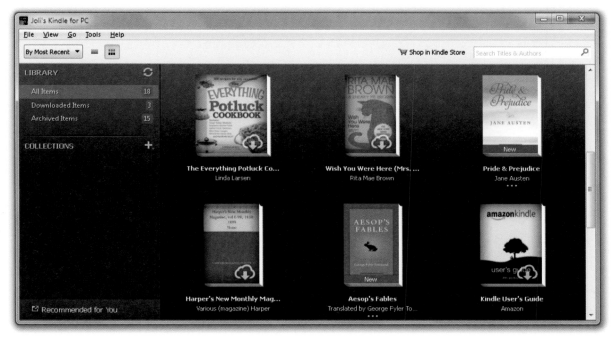

Figure 3-11: *The Kindle app for PC lets you read books on your computer.*

NOTE

If you aren't connected to the Internet when you use the Cloud Reader, you'll only be able to access books you've specifically called out for download to the computer you're using.

- You can purchase books easily and have them available on your Kindle the next time you use it.

- Once installed, like the Kindle Fire, you can download, navigate to, and read books; sort your library in various ways; and even configure personalized settings.

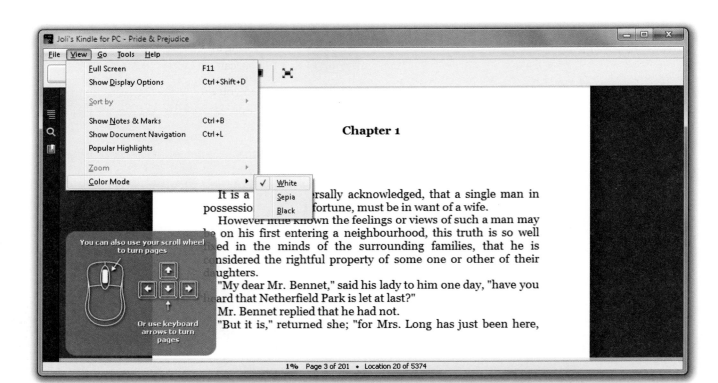

Figure 3-12: The Kindle app for PC and Mac offer features you'd expect to find.

Explore the Cloud Reader

The Cloud Reader is a web-based application, which means you don't have to download and install it like you do with the Kindle application. You simply navigate to www.amazon.com/cloudreader, sign in, and you'll be forwarded to the page shown in Figure 3-13. At this time, Cloud Reader only works with Apple Web browsers (Safari 5+ for Macs and Safari on an iPad running iOS4+)

USING OTHER DEVICES

If you have a compatible mobile device, you can download and install the Kindle app from the appropriate entity. On an Android device, use the Market; from an iPad, use the App Store; and so on. Once installed, open the app, log in, and explore it. It's important to note that the Kindle app for mobile devices does not include all of the available options you'll find on your Kindle Fire.

and Chrome, a Web browser from Google. If you don't have a Mac or iPad with the proper browser or operating system, Chrome is free and can be downloaded on any computer, even PC, as can Safari 5+.

After you've logged in—and you can do this from any computer, even one that isn't your own—you'll have access to all of your recently purchased books.

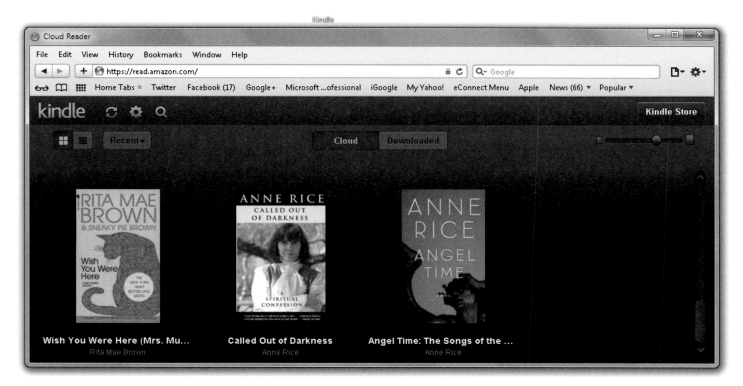

Figure 3-13: *After signing in to the Cloud Reader, you'll have access to your books.*

Chapter 4

Obtaining, Storing, and Listening to Songs and Audiobooks

Earlier Kindle models were, for the most part, simple e-book readers. Your Kindle Fire is much more than that. In this chapter, you'll learn that it's also a full-fledged MP3 and audiobook player.

Beyond being able to play music, though, the Kindle Fire comes with space in the cloud to store all of your Amazon music purchases for free, along with 5GB for storing your own data. Anything you opt to store there can be accessed on other mobile devices and computers. You can also copy music currently stored on your computer to your Kindle Fire by transferring it with a USB cable. As you know, the Kindle Fire comes with about 6GB of device storage space for your personal data, which means you can store a lot of songs on your Kindle Fire.

In this chapter, you'll learn how to obtain, listen to, and manage songs and audiobooks from and on your Kindle Fire. Interspersed throughout, you'll also learn how to incorporate other devices, the cloud, and even your personal computer for added flexibility.

Get Your Music on Your Kindle Fire

If you have music on your personal computer, you may want to copy those files to your Kindle Fire. If those music files are yours (meaning you purchased them outright), if they are a compatible file format, and if they are DRM-free (meaning there are no copyright limitations placed on them), you can manually copy them to your Kindle Fire and play them on it. You can also opt to upload your favorite music to your space in the cloud, using Your Cloud Drive Music, detailed later in this chapter, if you'd rather not perform this sync using USB.

Know Compatible File Types

There are several types of files that you can transfer and play successfully on your Kindle Fire. These include various types of non-DRM AAC, MP3, MIDI, OGG, WAV, and a few others. You'll learn more about these acronyms shortly. For the most part, you'll be transferring, copying, and buying MP3 and AAC files. If your music files aren't in a compatible format, you'll have to obtain software to convert them before transferring them from your computer to your device.

You can find the file format of a song that's stored on your computer using many methods. One is to right-click the file (on a PC) and choose Properties. Figure 4-1 shows an example of what you'll see when you do. Sometimes you can hover the mouse over a song title to view information about it.

Here's a little more information about the compatible file types:

- **Non-DRM AAC** AAC (Advanced Audio Coding) is the format of the music sold in Apple's iTunes store. These files end in .M4a (see Figure 4-1).

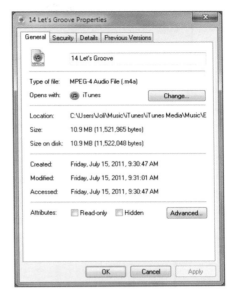

Figure 4-1: The Properties page for a file shows its file format.

- **MP3** MP3 (Moving Picture Experts Group Layer-3 Audio) is the format of the music sold in Amazon's MP3 Store (Music store). These files end in .mp3.

- **MIDI** MIDI (Music Instrument Digital Interface) is the format used quite often when music is created by connecting musical instruments to a computer, playing those instruments, and then saving the recording. These files end in several different extensions, including but not limited to .mid, .smf, and .kar.

- **OGG** (or OGG Vorbis) This is a newer file format that is roughly comparable to MP3 and AAC, among others. It is free, open, and unpatented, which distinguishes it from other common file formats. You probably won't have any OGG files to transfer.

- **WAV** WAV (Waveform Audio File Format) is the format used to save system sounds, like you hear when your computer starts up. However, you may have entire songs stored in this format too. These files end in .wav.

REVIEWING STEPS
FOR TRANSFERRING DATA

To copy music that's on your computer to your Kindle Fire:

1. Connect your Kindle using the available USB cable.

2. On a PC:

   a. Click **Start**.

   b. Click **My Computer** (or **Computer**).

   c. Open your Kindle Fire in the resulting window.

   d. Open the **Music** folder.

3. On a Mac:

   a. Open **Finder**.

   b. Select your Kindle Fire in the left pane under Devices.

   c. Open the **Music** folder.

4. Position this window to take up half of the screen.

5. Open a similar window on your computer, and browse to the location of the music you want to copy. Position this window to take up approximately half the screen.

6. Check the file type to make sure it's compatible (Windows Media Audio is not). Often, you can hover the mouse over a file to see this, as shown here.

♪ 02 so you want to be a rock n roll star
♫ 02. Graceland
♫ 02. Helplessly Hoping   Item type: MPEG Layer 3 Audio
♫ 02. Juke Box Hero   Size: 4.43 MB
♫ 02. LikeARock   Contributing artists: Paul Simon
♫ 02. Ramblin' Man   Length: 00:04:50

7. Using any method you're familiar with, copy the desired files to the Music folder on the Kindle Fire. Dragging-and-dropping is a common way to transfer files.

8. Wait until all of the files are copied, and then disconnect your Kindle Fire.

Once you've copied some music and disconnected your Kindle Fire, check to make sure the music is there.

1. On your Kindle Fire, navigate to the **Home** screen.

2. Tap **Music**.

3. Tap **Device**.

4. Tap **Artists**, **Albums**, or **Songs** and verify the songs are there, shown in Figure 4-2.

5. If desired, navigate to a song, tap the **Play** button, and then tap the **Pause** button to get a feel for the basic controls.

Figure 4-2: You'll find music you've copied under Device in Music.

Remember, if you'd rather not copy songs manually from your computer to your Kindle Fire, you can upload them to Your Cloud Drive Music from your computer, store them there, and access them from your Kindle Fire over

NOTE

For now, the album art associated with a music file isn't transferred with the music file, so you won't have art for your transferred titles in your Music library.

NOTE

To delete a song or album from your Kindle Fire, tap and hold it. From the resulting list, tap the applicable "Remove" option. You'll explore these options later in the chapter.

NOTE

Throughout this chapter, the focus will be on your Kindle Fire, but in various places you'll learn how to use other devices, including your computer, to access and manage your music.

the Internet. For more information about this, refer to the section later in this chapter titled "Upload Your Music to the Cloud."

Buy Music from Amazon

If you don't have any music to transfer, or if you want to purchase more, Amazon makes it easy. You can access and make purchases from the Amazon MP3 store from your Kindle Fire. It's almost as easy from your computer, a smartphone, an iPad, or an Android-based tablet, among others. Whichever you choose, once you purchase music from Amazon, you'll be able to access it from your Kindle Fire when you're ready for it there.

In this section, you'll learn how to purchase music from a Kindle Fire that's connected to a Wi-Fi network (and the Internet). To get started, tap Music on the Home screen, shown in Figure 4-3. If you opted to play a song in the previous section, you'll see that song listed on the Carousel.

Figure 4-3: Music lets you access media stored in the cloud and on your Kindle Fire.

Navigate the Amazon Music Store

After you tap Music on the Home screen, you'll have access to more items, including the Store. Many options you're already familiar with, including the Cloud and Device tabs (see Figure 4-4).

Figure 4-4: Store is an option once inside the Music section of your Kindle Fire.

- **Cloud**   Tap to access the music you have stored on Amazon's servers on the Internet, on Your Cloud Drive Music.
- **Device**   Tap to access the music you have specifically downloaded, copied, or stored on your Kindle Fire.
- **Store**   Tap to access the Amazon Music store.
- **Playlists, Artists, Albums, Songs**   Tap to sort the music by playlist, artist, album, or songs.

Tap Store now. Once inside the store, you can easily browse the available categories. These categories are shown in Figure 4-5 and include the following:

- **Featured**   Tap to see what's recommended for you. Once there, you have access to two tabs: Albums and Songs. You can also access daily deals. Flick and scroll to see more.
- **Bestsellers**   Tap to access a list of albums or songs that are the most popular at the moment. (Tap the Back button to return to the previous screen.)
- **New Releases**   Tap to see what's new, and sort by albums and songs. (Tap the Back button to return to the previous screen.)
- **Genres**   Tap to sort music by genre. There are too many to list here, but options include Blues, Children's Music, Classic Rock, Folk, and Soundtracks. (Tap the Back button to return to the previous screen.)

Figure 4-5: When you first enter the store, sorting options are available.

You can also search for something specific. You can search by song title, album, artist, and more.

1. From the Home screen, tap **Music**.

2. Tap **Store**.

3. Tap in the **Search Music Store** window and type your keywords. (If you'd like to download something but don't want to make an actual purchase, type **Free Music**.)

4. On the keyboard, tap **Search**.

5. Tap any result in the list to learn more or make a purchase. (Don't tap the price just yet.)

TIP

There is some free media at the Music store. If you're not ready to make a purchase, search for "free music."

CAUTION

If you opt to save your media purchase to your device instead of the cloud, your purchase won't be stored in the cloud. This means you're responsible for backing it up, and if you lose it (perhaps your device is stolen or damaged), you can't download it again.

NOTE

After making a purchase from the Music store, your music will be available under the Cloud tab of your Music library. If you want to download the music to your Kindle Fire, that's another step. Refer to the section "Download Music from the Cloud" later in this chapter to learn how.

Purchase Songs from Your Kindle Fire

Whether you want to make a purchase or download a song for free, the process is the same. You simply navigate to the media you want, tap a few times, and the music is yours.

When you're ready to obtain a free song or album or make a purchase:

1. From the Home screen, tap **Music**.
2. Tap **Store**.
3. Navigate to a song you want to purchase using the techniques outlined earlier.
4. Tap **Free** and then tap **Get**, or tap the price icon and then **Buy**, as applicable.
5. You may see an option that asks if you want to Save To Cloud or Save To Device. For now, save the music to the cloud.
6. Wait while the song downloads to Your Cloud Drive Music. See Figure 4-6.

Figure 4-6: Once a song or album has downloaded, you have the option to continue shopping or go to your music library to play the music.

Purchase and Download Songs from Your Computer

If you don't have a Wi-Fi network to connect your Kindle Fire to, you won't be able to shop for music from it. You'll have to shop from your computer. You may rather shop from your computer, however, perhaps because what's available in the store is easier to see, easier to access, or easier to navigate, even

QUICKSTEPS

BUYING MEDIA FROM YOUR COMPUTER

To purchase music on your computer:

1. Visit www.amazon.com.

2. Locate the MP3 Music store.

3. Browse the store until you find something you want. Click **Buy MP3**, **Get MP3**, or another option, as applicable.

4. If prompted, agree to the Terms of Use and click **Continue**.

5. Choose either **Save To Your Amazon Cloud Drive** or **No, Thanks, Only Save To This Computer**. Saving to the Cloud Drive is recommended.

6. Note that to play your purchased music at your computer, you may need to download the Amazon Cloud Player, detailed later in this chapter.

if you can connect your Kindle Fire to a Wi-Fi network. Whatever the case, shopping from a computer is an option, no matter what your Wi-Fi situation.

When you shop from your computer, you must somehow make the music you purchase available on your Kindle Fire. If your Kindle Fire has access to a Wi-Fi network, you can store what you buy in the cloud and either play it from the cloud or download it. If your Kindle Fire does not have access to a Wi-Fi network, you'll have to store the music on your computer and transfer it manually by connecting the two. If you're unsure when prompted where to save the music you buy from Amazon, here are a few tips to help you decide. Figure 4-7 shows what Your Cloud Drive Music looks like from a Windows-based PC.

Store purchased media on Amazon's Cloud Servers when you have the ability to connect your Kindle Fire to the Internet *and* when

- You want to access the media from your Kindle Fire or from an iPad, Android phone, or other compatible device but don't want to store it there.
- You do not want to worry about backing up your media yourself.
- You do not care about burning CDs of the media you buy.
- You are buying media using someone else's computer.
- You are concerned about the security of your media. Cloud storage is more secure than local storage.

Figure 4-7: Your Cloud Drive is separated into folders; this is a sample Music folder.

Store the media you purchase from Amazon on your own computer when you

- Have a Kindle Fire that does not have access to a Wi-Fi network.
- Only want to transfer, manually select, or otherwise make available certain songs to your Kindle Fire and want the rest to remain on your computer.
- Want to burn CDs of the music you buy.
- Want to transfer the songs to a portable media player that does not have Internet access.
- Want to listen to the music and create playlists using Windows Media Player or iTunes.
- Want better quality, want to be able to play more file types (such as Windows Media Audio), want to share your music over your home network, or want to play your media on a media player in your home, among other things.

TIP

To access music stored on Your Cloud Drive on a compatible device (other than the Kindle Fire), you must install the Amazon Cloud Player on it.

Use Your Free Cloud Drive

If you've purchased music and opted to store it on Your Cloud Drive Music, you can access that music from a long list of devices. What's stored there will be available on your Kindle Fire, of course, but it can also be made available to almost any PC or Mac computer, the Apple iPad, and various Android mobile phones and tablets. Here we'll focus on accessing your cloud data from the Kindle Fire, but later you'll learn how to access your music from other places.

Access Music Stored in the Cloud from Your Kindle Fire

If you've worked through this chapter from the beginning, you probably have some music stored on your Kindle Fire and some stored in the cloud. If you've made purchases from your Kindle Fire from the Amazon Music store or obtained any free music from there, you certainly have music stored in the cloud. In this section, you'll learn how to access the music you have stored in the cloud from your Kindle Fire. While you're there, you can also see what's on your device. After our discussion of the cloud is over, you'll learn how to play and control the music you own.

To access the music you have stored in the cloud from your Kindle Fire:

1. From the Home screen, tap **Music**.
2. Tap **Cloud**.
3. Tap **Artists**, **Albums**, or **Songs**.

Upload Your Music to the Cloud

You already learned how to manually copy music you own to your Kindle Fire by connecting it to your computer and copying the songs to it. When you do this, you use some of the available 6GB or so of free space on your Kindle Fire. If you run out of space on your Kindle Fire, or if you have that space earmarked for something else, you can store that same music in the cloud instead. Amazon has set aside 5GB of space available for you to use for your personal data, including music you have stored on your computer.

To upload your music to Your Cloud Drive Music:

1. From your computer, visit www.amazon.com.
2. At the top of the page, click **Your Digital Items**.
3. Click **Your Cloud Drive Music**.
4. In the top-left corner, click **Upload Your Music**.
5. Follow the prompts to download and install the Amazon MP3 Uploader, accepting all of the default options.
6. After the Amazon MP3 Uploader has scanned your computer for compatible music, you'll receive a report similar to what is shown in Figure 4-8. Then, you'll have to decide what you want to do:

   a. **Upload all of your music**   This is a good choice if you don't have much media, enjoy listening to all of it, and want to make it all available from your Kindle Fire, or you are willing to purchase additional space from Amazon for a yearly fee. Be careful about bandwidth restrictions placed on your Internet connection by your Internet service provider (ISP). If you are unsure about restrictions, contact your ISP.

CAUTION

If you have a lot of media on your computer, it may take the Amazon MP3 Uploader quite a bit of time to scan it. You can opt to stop that scan, if desired, and browse your media manually.

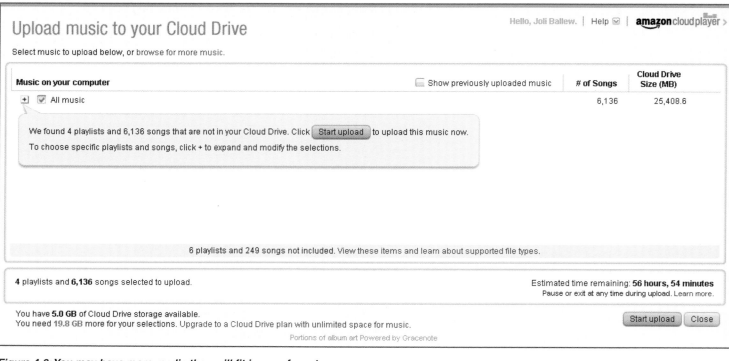

Upload music to your Cloud Drive

Select music to upload below, or browse for more music.

Music on your computer	☐ Show previously uploaded music	# of Songs	Cloud Drive Size (MB)
⊞ ☑ All music		6,136	25,408.6

We found 4 playlists and 6,136 songs that are not in your Cloud Drive. Click [Start upload] to upload this music now.

To choose specific playlists and songs, click + to expand and modify the selections.

6 playlists and 249 songs not included. View these items and learn about supported file types.

4 playlists and **6,136** songs selected to upload.

Estimated time remaining: **56 hours, 54 minutes**
Pause or exit at any time during upload. Learn more.

You have **5.0 GB** of Cloud Drive storage available.
You need **19.8 GB** more for your selections. Upgrade to a Cloud Drive plan with unlimited space for music.

[Start upload] [Close]

Portions of album art Powered by Gracenote

Figure 4-8: You may have more media than will fit in your free storage area.

b. **Upload some of your music**   This is a good choice if you have more media than will fit on your free space, do not want to purchase more, and/or do not want to make all of your media available on your Kindle Fire.

c. **Buy more storage space**   This is a necessary choice if you want to make more than 5GB of music available from the cloud and on your Kindle Fire.

7. Depending on your decision in step 6, you will have to do one of the following:

   a. Upgrade to another Cloud Drive plan.

   b. Start the upgrade of all of your music.

   c. Click any available plus (+) sign (an example is shown here) and select the songs to upload by selecting or deselecting the check marks.

8. When you're ready, click **Start Upload** (shown in Figure 4-8).

Download Music from the Cloud

You can download the music stored only in the cloud to your Kindle Fire or your computer's hard drive. If you do download something you've purchased, it'll still be available in the cloud; downloading a file does not remove it. The same is true of items you've uploaded.

To download music from the cloud to your Kindle Fire:

1. From the Home screen, tap **Music**.
2. Tap **Cloud**.
3. Locate the item you want to download. It can be a single song, an entire album, all songs by a particular artist, or a playlist you've created. Tap this and then tap the appropriate Download option. Here, that's **Download Album**.

4. You can watch the progress of the download by tapping the **Menu** icon and then tapping **Downloads**. Or you can simply wait for the media to appear under the Device tab.

STORING OTHER KINDS OF DATA IN THE CLOUD

You know that you can store up to 5GB of personal music on Amazon's Cloud servers. However, you may not know that you can store more than music. You can also store personal documents, pictures, and videos, among other things. What does this mean to you? For starters, provided your Kindle Fire is connected to the Internet via Wi-Fi when you need to retrieve your files and that they are of a compatible format:

- You can upload travel documents from your computer, and they'll be available on your Kindle Fire should you need to access them at the airport.

- You can upload a map or directions, a list of phone numbers or addresses, or other information as desired.

- You can upload your favorite photos to share with others from your Kindle Fire.

- You can upload your favorite (short) videos to show others, perhaps of a child or grandchild, and show that video using your Kindle Fire.

To download music from the cloud to your computer:

1. From your computer, visit www.amazon.com.

2. At the top of the page, click **Your Digital Items**.

3. Click **Your Cloud Drive Music**.

4. Choose one of the following four sorting options. Use these tools to locate the item(s) you'd like to download:

   a. **Sort By Songs**   Place a check mark beside each song title you want to download. When ready, click **Download** (see Figure 4-9).

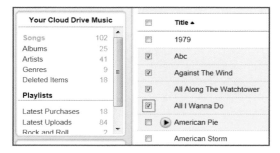

Figure 4-9: Use the sort option in the left pane to locate the item(s) you want to download to your computer.

   b. **Sort By Albums**   Hover your mouse over the album you want to download, click the down arrow that appears, and click **Download**.

   c. **Sort By Latest Purchases**   Place a check mark beside each song title you want to download. When ready, click **Download**.

   d. **Sort By Latest Uploads**   Place a check mark beside each song title you want to download. When ready, click **Download**.

5. If prompted to download or enable the Amazon MP3 Player for use with this browser and on this computer, do this. When the download and installation process completes, the selected songs will begin to download.

NOTE

If you tap the List View icon, the Back button, or the Search icon on the screen shown in Figure 4-10, you'll have to tap the Back button and/or song title that appears at the bottom of the page to return to that screen. Alternatively, you can tap the Menu icon at the bottom of the screen and tap Now Playing.

Listen to Music on Your Kindle Fire

To play a song on your Kindle Fire, you only need to tap it. Once a song is playing, various controls become available, including many you're probably already familiar with from using similar devices. You'll see Play, Pause, and Shuffle, among others. Figure 4-10 shows a sample screen.

If you don't see this screen but can hear music playing:

1. If you're on the Home screen, tap **Music**.
2. When in the Music app, if you still can't see the screen shown in Figure 4-10, tap the **Back** button and/or the song title at the bottom of the screen.

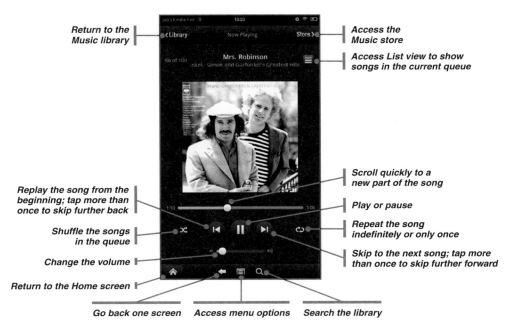

Return to the Music library

Access the Music store

Access List view to show songs in the current queue

Scroll quickly to a new part of the song

Replay the song from the beginning; tap more than once to skip further back

Play or pause

Shuffle the songs in the queue

Repeat the song indefinitely or only once

Change the volume

Skip to the next song; tap more than once to skip further forward

Return to the Home screen

Go back one screen   Access menu options   Search the library

Figure 4-10: The Kindle Fire's Music player has a lot of elements.

QUICKSTEPS

PLAYING A SONG OR ALBUM

To use the Music Player's controls, you must first locate a song and tap it. This generally requires scrolling through lists. To scroll more quickly, tap, hold, and drag the icon you see here. Once you've found a song to play in any screen or list, tap it once.

4:55

4:40

- To pause a song, tap the **Play/Pause** button.

- To skip to the next song, tap the **Next** button once. Tap more than once to continue skipping forward.

- To start the current song from the beginning, tap the **Previous** button once. Tap more than once to skip to the previous songs in the queue.

- To play the songs in a queue in random order, tap **Shuffle**.

- To change the view, tap the **List View** icon.

- To listen to music while performing other tasks on your Kindle Fire, tap the **Home** icon.

TIP

If you opt to play a song in any list, such as what you'll have if you play an album, the song after it will automatically start playing when that one is finished. This is true of any list, including any type of playlist you may create. To mix up the order, tap the Shuffle icon.

Create a Playlist

A playlist is a collection of songs that you group together or that are grouped together automatically based on similar characteristics. You might create a playlist list that contains fast songs you like to work out with, slow songs you like to have dinner by, or instrumental songs you like to have on in the background while you read. You can create playlists using the tools in the Music Player.

Here is one way to create your own playlist on your Kindle Fire.

1. From the Home screen, tap **Music**.
2. Navigate to a song you'd like to include in a playlist.
3. Tap and hold, and then tap **Add Song To Playlist**. (Note the other options.)

4. If this is your first playlist, tap **Create New Playlist**. (If you've created playlists already, you will see them here.)
5. Type a name for the new playlist.
6. Tap **Save**. See Figure 4-11.
7. Repeat this process starting with step 2. This time, when you tap and hold, you have the option to add the song to the newly created playlist.

8. To view and play the songs in the list, tap **Playlists**. You'll see Latest Purchases, Latest Uploads, and your new playlist.

TIP

Tap and hold any playlist to see more options, including adding more songs to it, renaming it, or deleting it.

Figure 4-11: Playlists hold songs that you select.

Here is another way to create playlists from your Kindle Fire.

1. From the Home screen, tap **Music**.

2. Tap **Playlists**.

3. Tap **Create New Playlist**.

4. Type a name for the playlist and tap **Save**.

5. In the screen that appears, tap the orange + sign by each song you'd like to add to the list. See Figure 4-12.

6. Tap **Done**.

7. The Download option will appear in the next screen; tap **Download** to download the playlist and songs to your Kindle Fire. Tap **Yes** when prompted. (Note the Edit option.)

8. Tap the **Back** button to return to the Playlists screen.

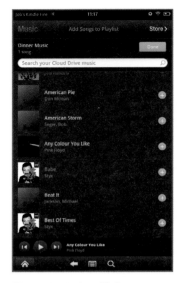

Figure 4-12: An efficient way to create playlists is to start from the Playlists tab and select multiple songs at once.

If you'd like, you can create a playlist on your computer at Amazon.com. You can then access this playlist on your Kindle Fire. To create a playlist from your computer and sync it to your Kindle Fire:

1. Navigate to www.amazon.com and click **Your Digital Items**.

2. Click **Your Cloud Drive Music**.

3. Click an option in the left pane (**Songs** is easiest for beginners), and place a check mark by a song you want in your new playlist.

4. Click **Add To Playlist**.

5. Type a name for the playlist and click **OK**.

6. Repeat to add more songs, selecting the new playlist each time you repeat step 4.

7. Note your playlist in the left pane. The next time you use your Kindle Fire while connected to the Internet, the new playlist will sync automatically and be available on it.

Explore the Menu Icon

You probably noticed the Menu icon at the bottom of the Music app. That Menu icon offers access to additional features and commands. Tap it to see the following, shown in Figure 4-13:

Figure 4-13: One option to explore now is Settings.

- Tap **Downloads** to view the progress of a current download or to see a list of completed downloads. From the Completed Downloads list, tap and hold any title to remove it from your Kindle Fire (to undownload it, as it were).

- Tap **Now Playing** to access the screen shown earlier in Figure 4-10.

- Tap **Settings** to view the various music-related settings. You can do a lot here, including entering a gift card claim code, locking the screen controls, and changing delivery preferences, among other things. There's more on this in the next section.

- Tap **Help** to access the Help files on Amazon.com.

Explore Settings

As noted in the previous section, when you tap the Menu icon in the Music app and then tap Settings, a slew of options appears. These are shown in Figure 4-14. Although they are easy enough to access, you may not fully understand what each option does.

Here's a quick summary of features available from Settings:

- **Enter A Claim Code**   Tap to enter the claim code on a gift card or one obtained through an Amazon promotion.

- **Clear Cache**   Tap to clear the data stored internally for songs in the Now Playing queue, album art, and similar metadata. You'll only need to do this if you've encountered problems playing music or viewing artwork.

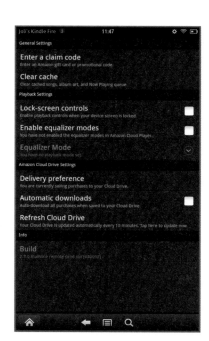

Figure 4-14: Some options, such as Refresh Cloud Drive, are more intuitive than Clear Cache.

- **Lock-screen Controls** Tap to enable playback controls even when you manually lock your device screen. By default, when you lock the screen from the status bar, all features are locked, even the playback controls.

- **Enable Equalizer Modes** When you enable this feature, the next one, Equalizer Mode, becomes available. Tap Equalizer Mode to select the desired playback options.

- **Equalizer Mode** When Enable Equalizer Modes is enabled, so is this. Tap to choose from various playback modes, including but not limited to Normal, Classical, Dance, Folk, Heavy Metal, Hip Hop, and Rock.

- **Delivery Preference** By default, purchases you make on your Kindle Fire from the Music store are saved to Your Cloud Drive. You can change this so all purchases are saved to the device to avoid having to download the media in a separate step. Changes you make here will be applied to all purchases, whether you make them on the Kindle Fire or through a web browser.

- **Automatic Downloads** Tap to enable automatic downloads. When this is selected, all purchases will be downloaded automatically to your Kindle Fire.

- **Refresh Cloud Drive** Tap to sync your Kindle Fire with Your Cloud Drive. By default, syncing occurs every ten minutes.

Obtain and Play Audible Content

Audible is company that is a subsidiary of Amazon.com, and they sell audiobooks. You can buy audiobooks outright, or you can become a member at www.audible.com and for a monthly fee, download a specific number of books based on the plan you choose. Audiobooks are a great way to "read" books when you are busy doing something else, like driving, shopping, walking, or just resting your eyes.

Purchase, Download, and Play Audible Content

You can obtain Audible content in various ways. You'll probably opt to purchase and download the desired content using your Kindle Fire. This is the most straightforward, and the capability is built right in. If you want to listen to the same content on another device later, you can often download it again using

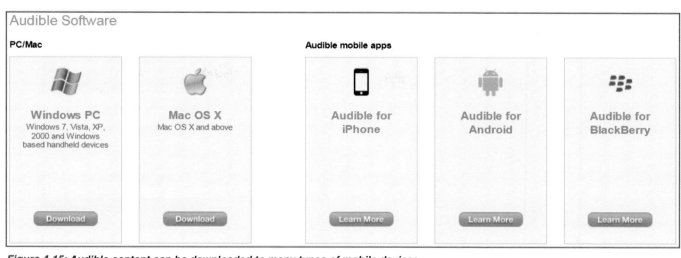

Figure 4-15: Audible content can be downloaded to many types of mobile devices.

TIP

If you have an Audible account, merge it with your Amazon account at www.audible.com/acc-merge. Then you'll have access to your subscription credits when you shop with your Kindle Fire.

the secondary device through an Audible app. Audible has apps for i-devices, Android devices, and even BlackBerry phones, and you can also download your content to your PC or Mac computer. Figure 4-15 shows the available software and information from Audible's website.

If you know you're going to want to burn CDs of your audiobooks, you may choose to purchase and download Audible content at your computer. With the files stored there, you can then burn CDs using your computer's own software and back up the files easily. You can also manually transfer the files to your Kindle Fire with a USB cable, but there's an app built in to your Kindle Fire that makes this unnecessary.

To get started with Audible from your Kindle Fire, or to simply explore the available content:

1. From the Home screen, tap **Apps**.
2. Tap **Audible**.

3. If you don't see the screen shown here, tap the **Menu** icon at the bottom of the page and tap **Shop**. (Shop isn't shown but the Menu icon is.)

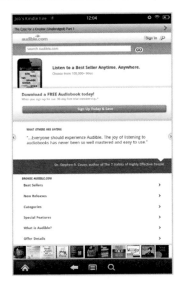

4. From here, you can sign up, sign in, shop, download a free audiobook, and more. It's up to you!

5. If you opt for a free audiobook, make a purchase, or become a member, the Audible app can be used to locate and play audiobooks.

If you listen to audiobooks you purchase on other devices, or if you want to burn CDs so you can listen to the books using your car's CD player, download the books directly from Audible.com to your computer. Later you can manually transfer the books from your computer to any device you want to listen to them on and download them from Audible to your Kindle Fire, when desired.

As with other apps, you can download media to your Kindle Fire. Once downloaded, you can then play the audiobook and have access to various controls. You can also tap and hold a title to access additional options. Figure 4-16 shows the Audible app in action. Note the Menu icon. As with other apps, this offers access to additional features like your Library, options to change the narrator's reading speed, options to sleep, and more.

Figure 4-16: The Audible app offers many of the same controls as the Music Player.

Manage Audiobooks

Audiobooks take up more storage space than e-books you download and read from the Amazon Book store. Thus, it's best to only keep the books you are actively listening to on it so that you'll always have room for other media as you acquire it. You may want to keep three to four audiobooks on your Kindle Fire at any given time, removing them when you're done, and downloading more when you're ready.

To remove any book you've downloaded to your Kindle Fire, as with other apps, simply tap and hold the title and, when prompted, opt to remove it from the device.

Chapter 5

Obtaining, Watching, and Managing Video

You can view various types of video on your Kindle Fire. You can watch movies, concerts, and recorded television shows from Amazon.com. You can watch videos others post online from websites like YouTube and CNN. You can watch personal videos you've posted to Facebook and similar websites; video you've copied to your Kindle Fire; and with the proper apps, television shows you missed, your home's security camera video stream, and live web cam video streams. If you've signed up for any third-party media subscription services and downloaded their related apps, you can watch media from companies like Netflix and Hulu too.

In this chapter, you'll learn what options are available from Amazon with regard to video, including how to access Amazon Prime Instant Videos, how to rent media titles, and how to buy them. You'll learn your options for watching that video too. After that, you'll learn how to view video through the web browser, view your personal videos in the Gallery (an app included with your Kindle Fire), and finally, how to sign up for and access Netflix and Hulu.

Become Familiar with Amazon Video

The Amazon Video store offers movies and television shows that you can watch on your Kindle Fire (and many other devices). This media is "streamed" to your device over the Internet. Streaming is a technology that allows video to be stored on Internet servers and sent to your device on demand, when you want it, and the data is sent wirelessly. Figure 5-1 shows the Video store as seen from the Kindle Fire.

Figure 5-1: *When you tap Video on the Home screen, you are taken directly to the Amazon Video store.*

A few things must be in place before you can access and ultimately watch Amazon Video store media. To access available video content to view, rent, buy, and possibly download to your Kindle Fire for viewing later (perhaps when you don't have Wi-Fi access), your device must be connected via Wi-Fi and registered to your Amazon.com account. In addition, to make purchases from the Amazon Instant Video store on your Kindle Fire, you must have an Amazon account with the 1-click payment option enabled. If you aren't sure if 1-click has been set up, or if you're sure it isn't, you'll need to enable it before continuing.

To set up your 1-click payment setting:

1. From a web browser, visit www.amazon.com and click **Your Account**.
2. Select the option that allows you to review or change your 1-click settings. (What you see can differ, depending on how your Amazon account is currently configured.)
3. Verify that mobile 1-click settings are turned on. You want to see what's shown here.

4. You must also have a valid credit card on file for making purchases. Input this information if prompted.

Browse Amazon's 10,000+ Prime Instant Video Titles

One of the first things you'll notice when you tap Video from the Home screen of your Kindle Fire is that the first entry in the Video store is *Prime Instant Videos,* and right next to that is a notice that says *$0.00 for Prime Members.* Under that are movies and television shows you can rent or buy. Take a few minutes to browse through the Prime Instant Video titles now. Then decide if becoming (or remaining) an Amazon Prime subscriber is right for you.

To browse the Instant Video store titles:

1. From the Home screen, tap **Video**.
2. In the first section, next to Prime Instant Videos, tap **View All**.
3. Verify that both **Prime** and **Popular Movies** are selected (both should be in orange), and scroll up and down to see what's offered. See Figure 5-2.
4. Tap **Recently Added**, tap **Editors Picks**, and then tap and drag Editor's Picks from right to left to see additional categories (All Genres, For The Kids, etc.).

NOTE

All new Kindle Fire owners have access to an entire month of Amazon Prime for free. Free trial members have access to everything paid members do, too, so you'll know exactly what you're getting with a membership while you explore (including access to the list of Prime Instant Videos). If you decide to keep it, it's $79 a year.

MANAGING YOUR
AMAZON PRIME SUBSCRIPTION

All new Kindle Fire owners receive a one-month free trial of Amazon Prime. With that subscription, you can watch over 10,000 movies and TV shows at no extra cost on your Kindle Fire and over 200 other devices, take advantage of free two-day shipping on millions of items sold on Amazon.com, and have access to the new Kindle Lending Library for books. If you were already an Amazon Prime member before getting your Kindle Fire, the transition is seamless.

- To learn more or manage your Amazon Prime membership, visit www.amazon.com from any web browser, and in the left pane tap (or click) **Unlimited Instant Videos**. Then select **Learn More About Amazon Prime**.

- Tap **Your Account** at the top of any Amazon.com page, and next to **Orders**, tap (or click) **Manage Prime Membership**.

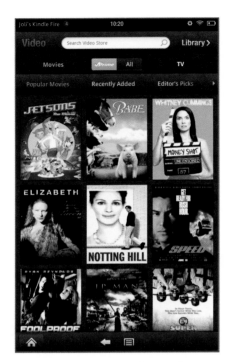

Figure 5-2: *While subscribed to Amazon Prime, you can watch all of the Prime Instant Videos for no additional charge.*

Amazon Prime Instant Videos cannot be transferred via USB from your computer to your Kindle Fire. All Amazon Instant Videos must be downloaded to your Kindle Fire by tapping **Download** in the Video app.

5. Tap and drag any category title back to the right to access Popular Movies once more.

6. Now, tap **TV**. It's located to the right of All. Repeat step 4 to view each category.

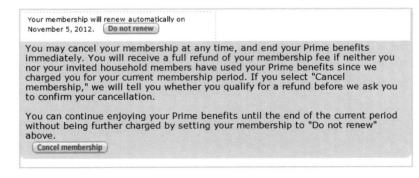

Your membership will renew automatically on November 5, 2012. **Do not renew**

You may cancel your membership at any time, and end your Prime benefits immediately. You will receive a full refund of your membership fee if neither you nor your invited household members have used your Prime benefits since we charged you for your current membership period. If you select "Cancel membership," we will tell you whether you qualify for a refund before we ask you to confirm your cancellation.

You can continue enjoying your Prime benefits until the end of the current period without being further charged by setting your membership to "Do not renew" above.

Cancel membership

Watch Amazon Video on Your Kindle Fire

In this section, you'll learn how to watch streaming video on your Kindle Fire. To work through the exercises here, you'll either need to be an Amazon Prime member or still be in the free trial period so that you can access the available free movies and TV, or be in a position to rent or buy a media title from Amazon.

Find a Movie or TV Show in the Amazon Instant Video Store

As you learned in the previous section, literally thousands of Amazon Instant Video titles are available from the Video store, and more and more are added all the time. You can choose from movies; TV episodes; and even concerts, documentaries, and recorded comedy. Your goal in the upcoming exercise is to find a media title you'd like to watch, either by browsing or searching. Once you've found it, you'll explore your options for obtaining it. You may be able to watch it for free with a Prime membership, or you may have to rent or buy it, depending on the media you've selected. Following that, you'll learn how to play and pause media, and later, how to control playback.

To locate a media title that interests you, from your Kindle Fire:

1. From the Home screen, tap **Videos**.
2. Using the techniques outlined in the previous section, browse the items listed under Prime.
3. Tap **All**.
4. Explore what's listed under Movies and TV. TV is shown in Figure 5-3.
5. Tap any entry to see the viewing and/or purchasing options. Figure 5-4 shows an entry for the TV series *Bones*. Note that you can only buy it. This particular series is not available to view for free with a Prime membership, and it isn't available for rent either.
6. To search for a specific title, tap inside the **Search Video Store** window and type the name of the movie or TV show.
7. Tap any item in the results to locate the product page.

CAUTION

Some product pages offer a button titled More Purchase Options. To see these additional options, tap **See All**.

Figure 5-3: When you view what's listed under All, you'll see everything that's available, not just what's offered with a Prime membership.

Figure 5-4: Some media is only available for purchase.

Choose Prime Instant Video, or Rent or Buy

If you're an Amazon Prime member and you select a media title that is free with your membership, all you have to do is navigate to the video's Product Page and tap Watch Now. An example is shown in Figure 5-5. (If you really like it and want to own it, you can often purchase it as well.) If you are not a Prime member, or have selected a movie or TV episode that isn't on the Prime Instant Videos list, then you'll have to rent or buy it.

Figure 5-5: **Tap Watch Now to start a free Amazon Prime Instant video.**

When you buy a movie, you can opt to watch it now or later. If you choose to watch it later, you'll want to download it to your device. If you buy the title, it's yours and you can watch it as often as you like, whenever you like. Figure 5-6 shows the movie *Star Trek*, which has been purchased, and appears in the Video Library on the Kindle Fire.

Figure 5-6: **When you buy a movie or TV episode, that title will always appear in the Kindle Fire's Video Library under the Cloud tab (you can download it to your Kindle Fire if desired).**

With rentals, there's a specific amount of time in which you can start to watch the movie, and once started, a specific amount of time in which to finish, depending on the device you rent it from and how rights have been applied by the publisher. When you rent a movie on your Kindle Fire, most rental periods start the moment you start the download, and you have 24 hours to complete it. When you rent from a computer, you have up to 30 days to start watching, and the 24-hour period starts after you click Play. You may see other options, though, specifically if the movies are old or if there's a promotion currently in place.

To rent or buy a movie:

1. Locate the movie you want to rent or buy. If applicable, tap its icon to access its Product Page.

2. Review the pricing options. You may have to tap **See All** to see every option available.

3. Tap the desired pricing option. Tap **Buy** or **Rent**.

4. Once you've made the purchase, tap **Watch Now**, or tap **Download** to save the media to your device to watch later. If you download the title, it will appear in your Video Library under Devices as well as under Cloud. You'll have to return to your video library to watch it when you're ready.

CAUTION

Before you tap Buy or Rent, make sure you really want the media. It'll be yours once you do!

Play a Media Title

Media from the Prime Instant Video list, as well as media you purchase or rent from your Kindle Fire, are available instantly, hence the term Amazon Instant Video. As you know, all you have to do is tap Watch Now when the option appears. If, however, you decide to watch a media purchase later and you opt to download the title, you'll have to navigate to the Video Library folder to access it first. You'll learn how to do both here. Whatever the case, once a title is playing, you can manage playback with familiar video controls.

To play an Amazon Instant Video media title on your Kindle Fire, or to watch any rental or purchase immediately after paying for it:

1. Tap **Watch Now**.
2. Place the Kindle Fire in Landscape mode.
3. Wait while the media streams to your device.
4. Tap the screen to access the controls. Locate the volume slider in the top-right corner and drag to adjust the volume. Note the other features in Figure 5-7.

Figure 5-7: *Tap the screen while a movie is playing to access the controls.*

QUICKSTEPS

USING THE MEDIA PLAYER'S CONTROLS

Once a media title is playing, you can control it on your Kindle Fire in ways similar to how you control media on DVD players, DVRs, and other media players. To experiment with the media player's controls:

1. Tap the screen to show the controls.

2. Tap the ten-second rewind button to review the last ten seconds of video.

3. Hold and drag the volume slider to change the volume.

4. Tap the **Play/Pause** button to stop and start playback.

5. Hold and drag the hi-speed scrubber to move forward and backward in the movie quickly.

6. Tap the **Home** button to stop playback and return to the Home screen.

If you previously downloaded a movie or TV episode and want to watch it now, or if you made media purchases on other devices before you purchased your Kindle Fire and want to access them, you'll have to navigate to your Video Library.

1. From the Home screen, tap **Video**.

2. Tap **Library**.

3. To access media you've downloaded to your Kindle Fire, tap **Device**. Then tap **Movies** or **TV**. Here TV is selected.

4. To access all of the media you've purchased from Amazon, either recently or in the past, tap **Cloud**, and then tap **Movies** or **TV**.

5. Tap the media title you want to play.

6. Depending on the circumstances, in the next screen you may have to scroll to locate the item and tap the title again (specifically if you've purchased a single episode of a TV series).

7. Once you're at the Product Page, tap **Watch Now**, **Resume**, **Play From Beginning**, **Download**, or **Delete**, as applicable.

TIP

Delete titles you've purchased, downloaded, and watched when you're finished with them. Your Kindle Fire can only hold so much data, and you don't want to fill it up with media you've already seen.

TIP

You can navigate to your digital library on your Kindle Fire and play video right in the web browser, but the video will not be optimized for "mobile" and you won't have access to the playback controls you'll need. Playback through a web browser on a computer works great, however.

Manage Your Amazon Purchases and Rentals

If you are an Amazon Prime member and only watch the free instant videos available to you, you won't have any digital videos to manage. Amazon does not yet offer an "instant queue" where you can see a list of what you've recently watched, or create a list of instant videos you'd like to see. However, if you've purchased or rented movies, you'll see active media listed in your Video Library when online at Amazon.com. Although it's difficult to manage your digital video purchases from your Kindle Fire, as you can see in Figure 5-8, it is possible. You can more easily manage your media libraries from the web browser on a computer.

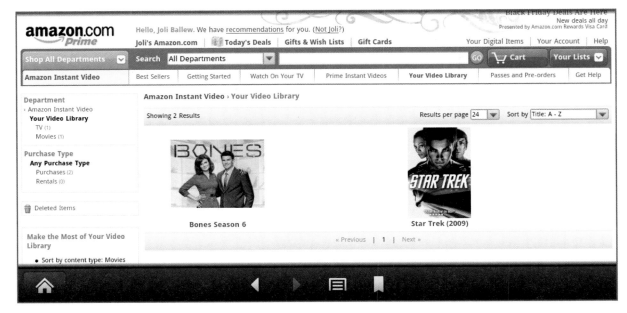

Figure 5-8: **You can manage your digital video purchase from any web browser, even Amazon Silk.**

Explore Your Video Library

However you get to your Video Library, once there you can perform actions on the video you own. You can delete an entire season of shows, a single episode, or a video from your library. If you choose to do the latter, the video will no longer be available for streaming to your Kindle Fire. You can restore it from the Deleted Items folder, though (unless you've emptied the contents of the folder since deleting the video), but it's best not to delete anything from your Video Library until you're positive you no longer want it.

To access your Video Library:

1. Using any web browser, navigate to www.amazon.com.
2. At the top of the page, select **Your Digital Items**.
3. Select **Your Video Library**.
4. Select any item in your library. Note that you can sort the items in the left pane.
5. Note the options; what you see may differ from what's shown in Figure 5-9.

CAUTION

Your Kindle Fire can only store so much data. If you're storing movies on it, try to keep fewer than eight or so at any given time to make sure you have enough room for other media.

Figure 5-9: *What you see when you select a title in your Video Library depends on what you select.*

DOWNLOADING A MEDIA PURCHASE TO YOUR KINDLE FIRE

By default, all of the media you purchase from Amazon is stored in the cloud on Amazon's servers. When you are ready to watch media you've purchased, you stream it to your Kindle Fire via the Internet. This is a good strategy, provided you're connected to the Internet with a strong Wi-Fi signal when you're ready to watch. However, you won't always have a Wi-Fi network to connect to. When you know you'll want to watch a movie and won't have a Wi-Fi connection, you should download that movie to your device while you're still connected to Wi-Fi. Once it's stored on your device, you can watch it whenever you want.

To download a movie or TV episode you've purchased to your Kindle Fire:

1. From the Home screen, tap **Video**.

2. Tap **Cloud**.

3. Tap **Movies** or **TV**.

4. Tap the item to go to its Product Page. If the item is part of a series, tap the episode you want to download.

5. Tap **Download**. Once the process completes, you'll see Downloaded, as shown here. (Make sure that the number of MB shown is not 0 or 1. If you see that, the download did not complete properly. If this happens, tap Options and download the item again.)

6. Tap the + sign by the title (if applicable) to see the option to download the item. Tap the + sign by the Download options to see where you can download the item to. Your Kindle Fire isn't one of the options.

7. Make changes and exit these windows as desired.

View Amazon Instant Videos on Other Devices

You can watch videos you've rented and purchased, specifically those available in your Video Library, on computers and mobile devices that include a compatible web browser. You watch them over the Internet through that web browser. You can also watch movies from the Amazon Prime Instant Videos list there. If you'd rather not view your media in a web browser, you can download your purchases to your computer and watch them using Amazon's Unbox Video Player for PC. This player offers more controls and feels more like a media player than a simple web browser does.

Likewise, you can watch Amazon Prime Instant Videos, as well as video you've rented or purchased, on compatible televisions or on televisions connected to compatible media players. Those devices must be connected to the Internet and be capable of streaming Amazon Instant Videos, and must have access to your network to access media stored on network storage devices.

Because technology changes so quickly, and because updates are offered often for web browsers and applications, it's hard to create a list of everything that's compatible. Therefore, you can check to see if the devices and web browsers you use are compatible here:

www.amazon.com/gp/video/ontv/devices.

WATCHING AMAZON INSTANT VIDEO ON YOUR TV

To watch Amazon video on your TV, first verify you have a compatible media player, as outlined earlier. Connect and install it as required and turn it on. Then:

1. Use your remote to change the "source" to the media device. Try DVI, HDMI, Composite, or another option until your player appears.

2. Using the remote that works the device, navigate to the Amazon app.

3. Browse what's there, moving left, right, up, and down to locate the movie you want to play.

View Videos Stored on the Web

There are other videos to view on the Internet besides movies and TV episodes from Amazon. You can view videos from YouTube, from news sites like CNN, and even video shared on Facebook and similar social networking sites. Because your Kindle Fire supports various video file types, including Flash Media (that's a specific kind of web media that isn't supported by all devices, including the iPhone or iPad), you can view almost anything on the Web.

View Online Video with Amazon Silk

You don't know a lot yet about the Kindle Fire's web browser, Amazon Silk, but you've probably surfed the Web enough times on computers and other mobile devices to make sense of it. In this section, you'll use Amazon Silk to access websites like YouTube and CNN and to view videos on those sites.

To view a video on YouTube:

1. From the Home screen, tap **Web**.

2. Tap the **+** sign at the top of the screen.

3. From the bookmark list that appears, tap **YouTube**. It will appear somewhere on the screen. See Figure 5-10.

Figure 5-10: Amazon Silk offers some preconfigured bookmarks, and YouTube is one of them.

4. Explore the interface if desired. There are various views and an option to search, among other things.

5. Tap the icon for any video you want to view.

6. Tap the **Play** icon that appears.

7. As with other video, tap the screen to view the controls.

8. At the bottom of the page are familiar controls. Tap **Back** to return to any previous screen.

To view video from CNN:

1. Tap the **+** sign at the top of the Amazon Silk interface.

2. Tap in the **Search Or Type URL** field, and type **cnn.com**.

3. Tap **Go**.

4. Browse to a video on the page and tap it. Video stories often have a video camera icon beside them.

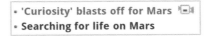

5. If applicable, tap the **Play** icon to view it; it will probably play automatically. The controls you'll see may only include Play/Pause and volume.

Experiment with other sites as time allows. If you have security cameras in your home and have previously been able to access those from a web browser for online viewing, try to log in and view those cameras now. Browse websites like ESPN, Facebook, and others that you know offer videos, and tap to view those too. Note that you may have to view a website in "Desktop" view to get to the videos you want to access because some "Mobile" webpage configurations don't offer access to all of the available content. You'll learn more about that in Chapter 8. Here you can see two videos posted to Facebook that can be played by tapping the Play icon.

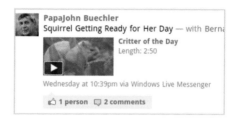

View Video Using the Gallery App

You can't play your personal videos within the Video Library on your Kindle Fire. You can, however, play personal videos that you've copied to your Kindle Fire from the Gallery app. You can open the Gallery app from the Apps tab on the Home screen. The types of video files the Kindle Fire can play are H.263 (.3gp, .mp4), H264 AVC (.3gp, .mp4), MPEG 4 SP/ASP (.3gp), and VP8 (.webm). You can also play videos sold by Amazon.com in the 60 Hz, NTSC format. This is the video format used in North America and Japan.

As with music files, you can right-click any file on your computer to see its file format prior to copying it.

If you find you have compatible personal video files on your computer, you can copy them to your Kindle Fire via USB. This process was outlined briefly in Chapter 1, and was detailed in more depth in Chapter 3 for transferring music.

WATCHING A PERSONAL VIDEO

You play personal video you've copied to your Kindle Fire from the Gallery app. After the video starts to play, you have access to familiar playback controls, including a volume slider, ten-second rewind button, Play/Pause button, and a hi-speed scrubber. To view a video in the Gallery app:

1. From the Home screen, tap **Apps**.

2. Tap **Device**, and then tap **Gallery**.

3. Tap **Video**.

4. Tap the video you want to play.

5. Tap the screen during playback to access the playback controls.

6. Note the **Back** button. Tap it to return to the previous screen.

Transferring video is similar, except you copy the files to the Video folder, not the Music folder. Once you have compatible personal video on your Kindle Fire, you can view it in the Gallery app.

To open and use the Gallery app:

1. From the Home screen, tap **Apps**.

2. Tap **Device**.

3. Tap **Gallery** to open the app. See Figure 5-11.

*Figure 5-11: **Use the Gallery app to view personal videos you've copied to your Kindle Fire.***

4. Tap **Video** to access them.

5. Tap and hold any video to access additional options, including Share, Delete, and More (this refers to the video's details). See Figure 5-12.

6. Tap **Share** to send the video via email; tap **Delete** to remove the video from your device.

7. Tap the **Back** button to return to the Gallery app.

Figure 5-12: *Videos in the Video section of the Gallery can be played if you see a thumbnail for them; otherwise, they are not compatible.*

Explore Other Media Options

There are options for watching professional video beyond streaming, buying, or renting from Amazon. You can get apps from the Appstore that let you watch video product reviews from companies like CNet, watch video trailers from entities like G4 to view sneak-peeks of new video games, and to watch movie trailers from various publishers of upcoming movies. E! Online offers an app that lets you watch clips of your favorite E! Television shows like *The Soup* and *Fashion Police*. As you can imagine, there are more and more of these apps arriving every day. You'll learn more about apps in Chapter 6. There are a couple of notable apps, however, that you'll want to explore right away if you are already a subscriber to Netflix and Hulu or are thinking about becoming a member.

Consider Netflix or Hulu Plus

Netflix and Hulu are two companies that offer streaming media. Both are compatible with your Kindle Fire, offer apps from the Appstore, and offer a free trial subscription. Once the required app is installed, you simply sign in with your account. Then, you can watch anything the company offers through their streaming services. Both services offer movies and television.

Figure 5-13 shows the Hulu Plus app's main screen. Although Free Gallery is an option, you will need to create an account and log in to use the app effectively.

*Figure 5-13: **Hulu Plus is an option for viewing TV and movies.***

Netflix is another option. As with Hulu Plus, you need to download and install the Netflix app, sign up and log in, and then you can access what's available for streaming. One of the options once logged in is Browse, and from there you can sort the video by genre. Here are some options for Sci-Fi & Fantasy.

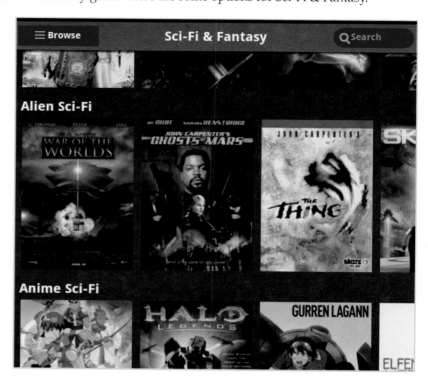

If you decide you'd like to give one of these services a try, the next chapter provides an optimal segue for you. While reading the next chapter, get the desired app, create an account, and log in. You may be amazed at what's offered!

How to...

Chapter 6
Exploring the Appstore for Android and Using Apps

You've likely experimented with a few apps by now. You may have explored a magazine app in Chapter 3; the Audible app in Chapter 4; the Gallery, Netflix, or Hulu Plus apps in Chapter 5; and others. You know you access those apps from the Home screen by tapping the Apps option. You probably know you can get more apps online. That's true; your Kindle Fire can run many of the apps created by developers for similar Android devices, at least the ones reworked for the Kindle and available in the Amazon Appstore.

In this chapter, you'll learn how to navigate the Appstore, buy apps, and download them. Then, you'll learn how to use those apps. Of course, your Kindle Fire comes with its own apps too, and you'll continue to explore those throughout this book.

Navigate to and Explore the Appstore

You know Amazon.com offers various sections where you can shop. Your Kindle Fire makes it easy to access related stores from the Home screen. So far, you've explored the Books store at Amazon.com (Books), the Music store (Music), and the Prime Instant Videos store (Videos). In this chapter, you'll explore another store, the Appstore. To get there, tap Apps on the Home screen, and then tap Store (see Figure 6-1).

Figure 6-1: **Tap Apps to access apps you've already downloaded or to shop Amazon's Appstore.**

Explore Appstore Categories

Once you've tapped the Apps button on your Kindle Fire's Home screen, you have the option to tap Store to enter Amazon's Appstore for Android. As with other online tasks, you'll have to be connected to the Internet to do this. Visiting the Appstore is a great place to learn about apps because it will help you understand very quickly what apps are and what's available before you start trying to acquire them.

To enter the Appstore from your Kindle Fire:

1. From the Home screen, tap **Apps**.

2. Tap **Store**.

3. Note the categories (Top, New, Entertainment, etc.), and tap any one of them. You'll see a new screen with new listings.

4. Tap the **Back** button to return to the main screen.

5. Repeat steps 3 and 4 until you've explored every category shown.

The available categories in the Appstore include:

- **Top** Tap here to see what apps are the top-selling ones at the moment. You'll see two options if you're viewing in Portrait mode, Top Paid and Top Free, shown here. Turn your Kindle Fire 90 degrees and you'll also see Top Rated.

- **New** This section offers brand-new apps in a new screen. Tap the **Back** button to return to the Appstore's main screen.

- **Games** Tap here to find games, and note the categories once there. You'll see Top, Action, Adventure, Arcade, and more. Tap and drag any category name from right to left to view more categories. You may see subcategories as you explore. For example, tapping Arcade under Games offers more sorting options, including Board, Cards, Casino, and others. Note the option to search for a game by its title.

- **Entertainment** Tap here to access apps like Netflix, Hulu Plus, E! Online, and similar entertainment options.

- **Lifestyle** Tap here to find apps that relate to lifestyle, like horoscopes, motivational quotes, personality tests, fun facts, thoughts of the day, and so on.

- **News & Weather**   This section offers apps that help you stay on top of news and weather. As with some of the other categories, News & Weather has subcategories, including but not limited to World, U.S., Newspapers, Sports, and Science. (Remember, tap the **Back** button to return to the previous screen.)

- **Utilities**   Tap here to access apps that provide a service or perform a task like Wi-Fi analyzers, battery savers, alarm clocks, calculators, and the like.

- **Social Networking**   Tap to access apps created by and/or for social networking websites.

- **All Categories**   Tap to access all categories, even those not listed. These include but are not limited to Books & Comics, City Info, Cooking, Education, and so on. Tap **Back** to return to the previous screen.

- **Recommended For You**   Tap to access apps you may be interested in, with recommendations based on apps you've previously purchased or used.

Locate Free Apps

There are lots of free apps, often by entities you recognize, like the Weather Channel, Adobe, and MapQuest. You will also find free versions of popular apps you'd normally have to pay for, which include advertisements for third-party products. Free apps, especially games, often prompt you regularly to buy the full app (and may do so as often as every turn of play). Free apps that offer motivational quotes, bible verses, daily affirmations, and the like may offer a group of, say, 30, and then charge you if you want to obtain more. Often, you'll have to upgrade a free app to its "paid" version to unlock the additional features you want as well. However, the free version of an app is a great way to decide if you like an app or not prior to buying it.

One way to locate free apps in any category is to opt to "refine" what's shown so that only free apps are offered.

1. Navigate to any category and/or subcategory, perhaps Games, and then Adventure.
2. Tap **Refine**.
3. Tap **Price**, which currently shows All, and tap **Free** from the resulting list. See Figure 6-2.

QUICKSTEPS

DOWNLOADING A FREE APP

Once you've found a free app you like, you can download and install it. You may want to read the reviews first, but you don't have to; you can just look at the number of stars it averages. You can download a free app from two places: from the list of apps or from its Details page.

1. From a list of apps:

   a. Tap **Free** beside the app you want to acquire.

   b. Tap **Get App**.

   c. When the download and installation completes, tap the **Back** button to continue shopping in the Appstore.

   > Thank you for purchasing this app.
   >
   > Downloading...

2. To access the app's Details page first:

   a. Tap the name of the app instead of the Free option.

   b. From the resulting Details page, tap **Free**.

   c. Tap **Get App**.

   d. When the download and installation completes, tap the **Back** button to continue shopping in the Appstore.

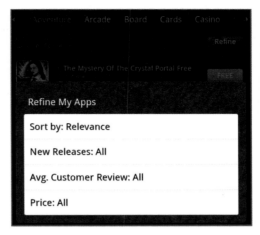

Figure 6-2: *Tap Refine on any screen to cull any list of results.*

To find free apps in the Appstore using other methods:

1. From the Home screen, tap **Apps**.

2. Tap **Store**.

3. Verify **Top** is selected, and then scroll through the **Top Free** list.

4. Alternatively, you can tap inside the **Search** window and type <u>free apps</u>. Then, tap the **Search** key on the keyboard.

Learn More About an App

You may be positive you want an app. Perhaps you know you want to play *Words with Friends* with family members, and you don't care what any reviewers have to say about it or how it's rated. Likewise, you may be sure you want the American Airlines app so that you can be notified of gate changes, flight delays, and estimated times of arrival, and again, what others have to say about it isn't important to you. You may already know what an app does and offers too, so you're not that interested in the details.

However, there will be times when you're on the fence about an app, and reading reviews and ratings will certainly help you decide. It may also be that the name of the app is enticing, but you're not quite sure what features it offers or what it does. In these cases, you'll want to visit the app's Details page. Figure 6-3 shows the Details page for *Angry Birds Free.*

Figure 6-3: *An app's Details page offers information about the app, including its features, user reviews, and the app's publisher.*

To access an app's Details page and navigate it:

1. Search for the desired app using any method.
2. Tap the name of the app (do not tap the Free or Price button).

3. A new page appears that enables you to obtain the app, save it, or share information about it via email. For now, simply scroll through the page and read the information offered.

4. Tap **Photos**, **Reviews**, and **Recommendations** to learn more about the app.

Buy and Download an App

You learned how to download and install a free app earlier in this chapter. The process is the same for buying apps. However, instead of tapping the Free icon, you tap whatever price is shown. For the sake of completeness, here are the steps to buy an app.

1. Using any method, locate the app you want to buy. You may want to search for an app, as shown in Figure 6-4.

Figure 6-4: *Although results will appear as you type in the Search window, often tapping an item there doesn't offer any apps; tapping Search on the keyboard is better.*

2. Tap the **Price** icon, either from the results list or the app's Details page.

SEARCHING FOR AN APP BY NAME

If you know the name of the app you want to obtain, you can search for it.

1. From the Home screen, tap **Apps**.

2. Tap **Store**.

3. Tap in the **Search In Appstore** window at the top of the page. Type the app's name or part of it.

4. If you see the desired result in the list, tap it. Note that this doesn't always produce results, though. It's often best to tap **Search** on the keyboard.

3. Tap **Buy App**. Be careful! Once you tap Buy App, it's yours!

4. Wait while the app downloads and installs.

View App Permissions

Apps require access to various parts of your Kindle Fire to function. At the very least, most apps need to access information about your current network connectivity. You can't send your latest *Hangman* word to another person over the Internet if you aren't online, for instance. Some require information about your current location to work properly. You can't get directions from your current location to the closest bar if the app can't determine where you are. Some apps even need access to personal information. That's why, when you search for an app to install, there's a list of the permissions required to run that application. Here's a complete list of items you may see, categorized by their type. If any of the items in this list make you uneasy, do not give the app permission to run.

- **Cost Money**   Used for permissions that can be used to make the user spend money without their direct involvement. This could prove to be a dangerous app to install.

- **Development Tools**   Group of permissions that are related to development features. Apps that require this are often okay to allow, provided you trust the publisher and the reviews seem good to you.

- **Hardware Controls**   Used for permissions that provide direct access to the hardware on the device. This is okay, provided the app is from a publisher you trust. Bad computer code can cause problems for devices that run them. Again, read the reviews for problems before installing.

- **Your Location**   Used for permissions that allow access to the user's current location. If you're concerned about your privacy and don't want any app on your Kindle Fire to know where you are, do not install apps that require you to give up location information. (Here this is listed in reference to GPS information.)

- **Messages**   Used for permissions that allow an application to send messages on behalf of the user or intercept messages being received by the user.

Application Permissions
- Read only access to phone state
- Write to external storage
- Open network sockets
- Change Wi-Fi connectivity state
- ACCESS_NETWORK_CHANGE
- Access fine (e.g., GPS) location
- Access the vibration feature
- Access information about Wi-Fi networks
- Access coarse (e.g., Cell-ID, WiFi) location
- Read the user's contacts data
- Access information about networks

This can be another potentially dangerous or annoying permission to allow, as posts may be automatically sent to Facebook or other players.

- **Network Communications**   Used for permissions that provide access to networking services. Most apps need access to a network to run, and this is generally one you don't have to worry about.

- **Personal Info**   Used for permissions that provide access to the user's private data, such as contacts, calendar events, email messages, etc. Only allow apps that require this if you're sure you want the app to have access to your personal information, and only if the app has gotten good reviews and is from a trusted publisher.

- **Phone Calls**   Used for permissions that are associated with accessing and modifying a user's telephony state: intercepting outgoing calls and reading and modifying the phone state. This is not applicable to your Kindle Fire.

- **Storage**   Group of permissions that are related to SD card access. The app may need to access your Kindle Fire's available storage space, and you'll have to allow it if so.

- **System Tools**   Group of permissions that are related to system APIs (application programming interfaces). As always, read the reviews and allow this only if you trust the app and its publisher.

Use Apps

You know now that apps are applications that run on your Kindle Fire and are stored there, and enable you to do things like check the weather, access breaking news, make a calculation, play a game, be productive, or follow a diet or exercise program, among other things. You choose the apps you want and need from Amazon's Appstore. Once that app has been downloaded to your Kindle Fire, you can open and use it.

Open Any App and Learn How to Use it

The first time you open most apps, an introductory screen appears offering instructions for use. If nothing is available with instructions, you'll often see an option to type your name, choose the number of players, watch a demo, enter data (like a starting weight), or perform some other task. Whatever you see, take some time to work through the introductions that are offered.

TIP

Newly acquired apps will appear first on the Home screen.

TIP

Most apps aren't terribly complicated to use (although games can be) and will offer helpful hints and suggestions as you use them.

In some instances when you open an app, a screen appears and it's as though the app maker assumes you have a good idea how to use it without instruction. MapQuest is one of those apps, but there are several icons on the screen that are intuitive, and the Menu icon offers options, including buttons to view a full map, get directions, clear the map, show traffic, and more. If you do not receive instructions, tap a few icons on the screen and you'll likely catch on quickly.

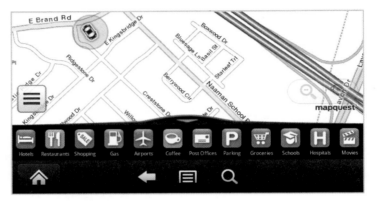

To see how your new apps respond, open them one at a time and see what's offered. You can open recently acquired apps from the Carousel on the Home screen, or you can tap Apps and sort your apps by Recent.

To open an app from Apps:

1. From the Home screen, tap **Apps**.

2. Tap **Device**. (All of your apps, including any you've acquired on other Android devices but not yet downloaded to your Kindle Fire, appear under the Cloud tab.)

3. Tap **Recent**. Figure 6-5 shows a sample screen.

4. Tap the desired app to open it.

5. If prompted, input introductory information such as your name, weight, age, and the like.

6. Read any introductions, and if available, read any instructions or Help files.

7. Tap the **Menu** button if it's available to see your other options. You may also see **Hints**, as shown here, or arrows that are available for more information. (In this game, you must tap the **Menu** icon to access the Back button to exit the game.)

PLAYING ANGRY BIRDS

If you have yet to get an app, for whatever reason, search for and obtain the free version of *Angry Birds*. You only need to know one gesture to play it, and the game becomes more and more challenging as you move through the levels.

1. From the Home screen, tap **Apps**.

2. Tap **Device**.

3. Tap **Angry Birds**.

4. Tap **Play** to start the game.

5. When an ad appears, tap the **X** on the ad to hide it.

6. Tap the first icon that appears, and then tap the **1**. This is the first level.

7. Tap the check mark to show you understand how to fling the angry birds.

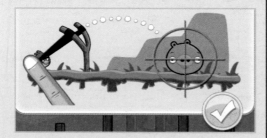

8. Tap and drag backward on the bird in the slingshot, and then let go to fling it.

9. Depending on your success or failure, tap to replay the level or move to the next level.

10. To exit the game, tap the up arrow at the bottom of the screen, and tap the **Home** icon.

*Figure 6-5: **Apps you've acquired from the Appstore appear under Device.***

Write a Review and Rate an App

Once you've used an app for a while, you may decide to write a review of it. What you write and how you rate the app will help others decide if they should get it or not. A good review states what is great about the app as well as what could use improvement. Of course, if the app doesn't do what it's supposed to, you should include that too! Often, you'll find that while an app is free, you must make a purchase to do anything with it. This is a sort of bait-and-switch, and is also worth mentioning in your review. Other times, the app is so inundated with ads that it is more annoying than useful. On the other hand, many free apps are quite useful, and not annoying at all!

To write a review from your Kindle Fire:

1. Locate the app in the Appstore. Be careful to find the exact app; there may be a dozen versions of the same app, or similarly titled apps.

2. Tap the app name to go to its Details page.

3. Tap the **Reviews** tab.

EXPLORING THE APPSTORE'S MENU ICON

While in the Appstore, tap the **Menu** icon to see the additional options. These include Categories, Recommended, My Subscriptions, My Apps, Settings, and More. The Categories and Recommended options simply do what their counterparts do on the Appstore screens, but others stand out:

- **My Subscriptions**   Tap to see what you're subscribed to. You may see a magazine that must be read through an app, for instance.
- **My Apps**   Tap to see three tabs: New, Update Available, and All. Tap Update Available to see if any apps need to be updated.
- **Settings**   Tap to apply gift cards, apply parental controls, and view release notes.
- **More**   Tap to see apps you've saved, recently viewed, contact customer service, leave feedback, or get help.

4. Tap **Create Your Own Review**.

5. Tap the desired number of stars to give the app, and then type your review.

6. Tap **Submit Your Review**.

Manage Apps

Apps can be more complex than you expect, and you can come to depend on them, become addicted to them, or use them often. You may come to depend on an app to keep track of your calories, your schedule, or even your children, and you may enjoy playing games alone or with friends regularly. You may post status updates or tweet several times a day, too, using an app you acquired from the Appstore. Of course, you can acquire and become bored with apps just as easily. Because apps can amass quickly, it's best to learn to manage them from the beginning.

Disable In-App Purchases

Many games have a depth to them that keeps you playing time and again by offering additional levels and new and greater challenges. Features are often "unlocked" as you move through the game and through existing levels of play. News and weather apps offer new and updated information regularly. And games, like *Words with Friends* and *Hanging Free*, continually prompt you to sign in with your Facebook account so you can find more and more people to play the game with. For the most part, these new features are free.

Many apps, to keep you engaged, offer items you can purchase to make the app more fun or useful. You may be able to purchase hints to solve puzzles, a new month of inspirational quotations, new horoscope entries, or a new list of foods with calories and fat included. Of course, your kids will want to add new characters, new games, and new music too. This can become expensive, and thus, you should be aware that it's possible to disable in-app purchasing. Even if you aren't sure you've ever run across this feature, it's best to disable it now.

1. From the Home screen, tap **Apps**.

2. Tap **Store**.

3. Tap the **Menu** icon and tap **Settings**.

4. Tap **In-App Purchasing**, shown in Figure 6-6.

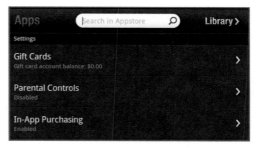

Figure 6-6: **In-App Purchasing is enabled by default; it may be best to disable it.**

5. Tap the check mark beside Allow In-App Item Purchases.

6. Type your Amazon account password. Tap **Continue**.

7. Tap the **Home** icon.

Update Apps

Apps are updated occasionally, and you should install those updates. Some updates fix problems, some add new functionality, and others add programs and features. Some updates address security issues. Part of managing your apps is acquiring these updates.

> **NOTE**
>
> Notice you can also set parental controls in the Appstore settings. If you have children who use your Kindle Fire unattended, consider enabling these controls.

To check for and install updates:

1. From the Home screen, tap **Apps**.
2. Tap **Store**.
3. Tap the **Menu** icon, and tap **My Apps**.
4. Tap **Update Available**.
5. If you see apps to update, tap **Install**. As you can see here, there are no apps to update at this time.
6. Tap the **Home** icon to return to the Home screen.

Remove an App from Your Kindle Fire

If you no longer want an app to appear on your Kindle Fire, you can remove it. Removing unused and unwanted apps frees up storage space. When you remove an app, the app is only removed from your Kindle Fire; it is not deleted from your digital library. You can download it again at any time. You won't have the option to remove built-in apps like Email or Contacts.

To remove an app from your Kindle Fire:

1. From the Home screen, tap **Apps**.
2. Tap **Device**.
3. Tap and hold for about a second on the app you want to remove.
4. Tap **Remove From Device**. See Figure 6-7.
5. Tap **OK**, and tap **OK** once more.

Figure 6-7: *Remove apps you don't use from your Kindle Fire.*

TIP

It's important to take inventory of what's stored on your Kindle Fire once a month or so. Make sure to remove anything you don't use so that when you run across something you want, you'll have room for it.

TIP

You can tap and hold any app to add it to Favorites on the Home screen.

If you decide later to reinstall the app and you have not deleted it from your digital library as outlined later in this chapter:

1. From the Home screen, tap **Apps**.

2. Tap **Store**.

3. Tap the **Menu** icon, and tap **My Apps**.

4. Tap **All**.

5. Locate the app and tap **Install**.

Explore Built-in Apps

Although you'll continue to explore the built-in apps as you work your way through this book, take a minute now to review what's installed. From the Home screen:

1. Tap **Apps**.

2. Tap **Device**.

3. Scroll to see apps that aren't displayed on the current screen.

4. Tap **By Recent** or **By Title**.

5. If you see an app you acquired from the Appstore that you know you'll never use, tap to remove it.

6. Tap **Cloud**.

7. Scroll to see what's available here. If an app has a down arrow on it, it's available for downloading.

8. Tap **Device** again.

9. Continue exploring as desired, opening apps if you like.

Chapter 7

Reading, Writing, and Managing Email

Your Kindle Fire comes with an email application built right in. With it you can retrieve email; reply to, forward, and compose new email (and add attachments); and mark email as spam. You can view your email in the Unified Inbox or one account at a time. The Kindle Fire can also be used to set up some email accounts automatically, including Google Gmail, Yahoo! Mail, Hotmail, and AOL. You can open and save attachments too, including Microsoft Word documents, Excel spreadsheets, and PowerPoint presentations, along with various kinds of images and video. In this chapter, you'll learn how to do all of this and more.

Set Up the Mail App

You've probably set up email accounts before, whether on a mobile phone, another tablet, or a computer. For the most part, you locate the option that enables you to input your email address and password, configure settings specific to your email provider if required, and wait while your email arrives in your inbox. It's a similar process on your Kindle Fire.

Identify Compatible Email Accounts

There are basically two kinds of personal email accounts. Web-based email accounts are those you get from entities such as Google, Yahoo!, AOL, and Hotmail, and they are almost always free. POP3 email accounts are those you get from Internet service providers like Time Warner, Verizon, and AT&T. Both types have their advantages and disadvantages, but one advantage of web-based accounts is that they are almost always natively supported on mobile devices (this means they are configured automatically after you input your email address and password). One disadvantage of POP3 accounts is that they are generally *not* natively supported, and you must manually input the required ports, servers, and security settings yourself.

Figure 7-1 shows the natively supported accounts. If you have an email account from one of these entities, setup will be simple:

- **Gmail** An email address from Google. You can get a free Gmail account at www .gmail.com.

- **Yahoo!** An email address from Yahoo!. You can get a free Yahoo! account at www .mail.yahoo.com.

- **Hotmail** An email address provided by Microsoft. Get a free Hotmail or Live account at www.hotmail.com.

- **AOL** An email address provided by AOL. You do not have to subscribe to AOL service to get a free address. Get a free AOL account at www.mail.aol.com.

NOTE

If you configure multiple email accounts, email for all of them will appear in the Unified Inbox, although you can sort email by a specific account if desired.

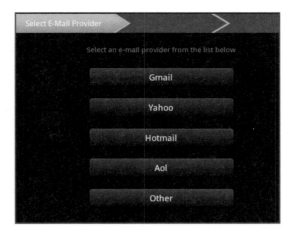

Figure 7-1: *When you set up the email application, you first choose the type of account you want to use.*

Set Up Your Web-Based Email Accounts

Setting up your web-based email accounts is easy. Once you've worked through the short set-up wizard, email for the configured account(s) will automatically arrive in your inbox. Contacts associated with natively supported accounts can be imported during the process as well.

CONFIGURE A NATIVELY SUPPORTED EMAIL ACCOUNT

To set up your Kindle Fire with a natively supported account from Gmail, Yahoo!, Hotmail, or AOL:

1. Tap **Apps** and tap **Email**.
2. Tap **Start**. (If you don't see Start, tap the **Menu** icon and tap **Add Account**.)
3. Tap the applicable option: **Gmail**, **Yahoo**, **Hotmail**, or **AOL**.
4. Type your user name. This is your email address.

5. Tap **Next** on the keyboard. You can see the keyboard here.

6. Type your password. See Figure 7-2.

Figure 7-2: You must input your user name and password to set up your email account.

7. Tap **Next**.

8. If you input your user name and password correctly, you'll be prompted to type a display name (the name that will appear on outgoing emails) and account name (like Gmail, Hotmail, Yahoo!, or AOL). If you see an error instead, follow the prompts to input the information again or correct it.

9. Review the checked items, uncheck any if desired, and tap **View Your Inbox**. See Figure 7-3.

TIP

To access the underscore character (_), tap it from the options that appear just above the keyboard. To access the _ on the keyboard, you'd have to do much more: tap the **123!?** key, tap the **.+=** key, and then tap **_**. Then you'd have to tap **ABC** to return to the main keyboard.

Figure 7-3: **You can opt to import contacts or set the account as the default during setup.**

Configure "Other" Email Accounts

If the email account you want to set up is not a natively supported one, you'll have to tap Other and input the details about your email account manually. The best thing to do prior to starting is to call your ISP or access its online Help pages to find out the following (note that it's not important you understand what any of this means or represents, only that you know the proper settings):

- **Server Type**   This will be IMAP or POP3.
- **Incoming Server**   This is the name of the server where your email arrives at your ISP.
- **Security Type** (for both incoming server and outgoing server)   This can be a number of things: SSL, TLS, or None, with specific settings like Always or If Available.

- **Authentication Type** (for both incoming server and outgoing server)   Your ISP may give you information about the authentication type, but you probably won't be prompted to input it during setup.
- **Incoming Port and Outgoing Port**   This could be a number of things, but is often 110, 993, 143, or 995.
- **Outgoing Server**   This is the server used for outgoing mail. Ask your ISP for the name of that server and any required authentication or port information required to go with it.

Once you have this information, you're ready to set up your email account using Other.

1. Tap **Apps** and tap **Email**.
2. Tap **Start**, and if you don't see that, tap the **Menu** icon and tap **Add Account**.

3. Tap **Other**.
4. Type your user name. This is your email address.
5. Tap **Next** on the keyboard.
6. Type your password. Tap **Next**.
7. Choose **POP3** or **IMAP**.
8. Input the correct settings for incoming server settings. What's shown is probably not correct. Tap **Next**. You will have to tap **Edit Details** if you receive an error and try again.
9. Input the correct settings for outgoing server settings. See Figure 7-4. What's shown is probably not correct. Tap **Next**. You will have to tap **Edit Details** if you receive an error and try again.
10. Tap the down arrow by Manually to configure how often you'd like to have your Kindle Fire check for email. You can select Every 15 Minutes, Every 30 Minutes, or Hourly (or leave at Manually). Tap **Next**.
11. Type a display name (the name that will appear on outgoing emails) and account name (like Time Warner or Verizon).
12. Check **Send Mail From This Account By Default** if desired, and then tap **View Your Inbox**.

CAUTION

If you receive an error that your user name or password is incorrect and you've corrected it and are still receiving the error, retype both from scratch.

NOTE

If you decide that setting up these "other" accounts is just too much to deal with, you can forward all mail to a natively supported address instead, although it's anything but an ideal solution.

TIP

If you can't get your non-web-based email accounts configured on your own, call your ISP or refer to Amazon's Help pages.

TESTING EMAIL ACCOUNT SETTINGS

If you made it through the various email set-up processes without errors, it's highly likely you'll be able to send and receive email without any problem. However, problems have been known to occur, and sometimes forwarded email (if you're configured it) doesn't arrive when and where you'd like. Thus, it's best to test your configured email accounts from all angles, just to be sure. Here are a few tips for testing:

- Send an email from each account you configured on your Kindle Fire back to that account and verify it arrives successfully on it.

- Delete just-arrived, web-based email on your Kindle Fire and verify the email still arrives in other places, including the email program you use to retrieve the mail on your computer and at the email provider's website.

- Send an email from any POP3 email account you've forwarded back to that POP3 account. Verify that the email arrives both on your Kindle Fire and on any computers you use.

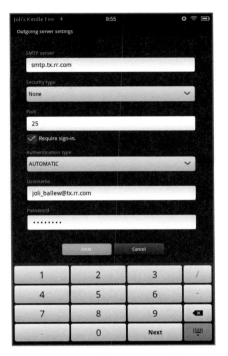

Figure 7-4: *Input the proper settings as noted by your ISP.*

Open, Locate, and Manage Incoming Email

The first thing you'll want to do after configuring your email accounts is check for new email and respond to it. You may also want to mark an email as spam, delete email, start and save an email for completion later, and perhaps even open or save an attachment.

Check for and Read New Email

When you set up your email accounts on your Kindle Fire, specific settings were configured by default. One of those was that you'd receive email manually, only when you check for it. Unless you were prompted and changed that setting during setup, you'll have to open the Email app to retrieve your email; your email will not arrive automatically while the Kindle Fire is asleep. To check for mail, you can either navigate to the appropriate account inbox after opening the Email app, or, while using the app and while in any inbox, tap the Refresh button shown here.

To check for email in the Unified Inbox where email from every configured email address arrives:

1. From the Home screen, tap **Apps**.
2. Tap **Email**. (You should also be able to tap **Email** from the Carousel.)
3. Tap the arrow by **Unified Inbox**. Mail will be retrieved automatically when you do.

4. If you're in some other inbox, tap the arrow beside it, and then tap **Unified Inbox**. (This is not shown.)
5. If you've been in any inbox for a while, tap the **Refresh** button to check for email again.
6. Tap any email in the list to read it.
7. Tap the **Trash** icon to delete it.

Locate a Specific Email

Sometimes you need to locate a specific email. This can prove difficult when the email you're looking for isn't a recent one and you have too many emails in the list to find the one you want quickly. In these cases, you'll want to sort the emails to cull what's shown.

One way to sort emails is to move away from the Unified Inbox and access a specific inbox for a single account instead. This can be quite helpful if you have a personal account that only your closest friends and family know to use and you're looking for an email one of them sent to that account, or to get away from a long list of emails from LinkedIn, Facebook, and other websites you configured with a specific email account created for that purpose. To access a specific email account's inbox, tap the arrow beside the Unified Inbox (or whatever inbox is shown), and tap the inbox you'd like to view.

Figure 7-5: *Change the sorting options to reconfigure how the list of emails is shown.*

By default, emails are listed in a specific order, with the newest emails listed first. To find an email using a different characteristic, sort the entries by the sender, the subject, or some other option. To change the sorting options in any inbox:

1. Tap **Newest**.

2. Tap any other option. See Figure 7-5.

Finally, to find something specific, tap the **Search** icon on the Options bar at the bottom of the screen. Then, in the resulting Search window, type your keywords.

Save an Attachment

If what's attached to an email is of a compatible file type, you can save the attachment to your Kindle Fire and access it later. When you do, you can delete the email it was originally attached to. Compatible file types have already been discussed in this book, but for the most part, when email is involved, you'll

NOTE

Images embedded in the body of an email appear as a placeholder until you tap Download Complete Message.

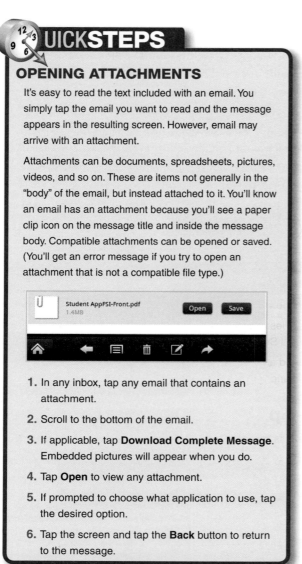

QUICKSTEPS

OPENING ATTACHMENTS

It's easy to read the text included with an email. You simply tap the email you want to read and the message appears in the resulting screen. However, email may arrive with an attachment.

Attachments can be documents, spreadsheets, pictures, videos, and so on. These are items not generally in the "body" of the email, but instead attached to it. You'll know an email has an attachment because you'll see a paper clip icon on the message title and inside the message body. Compatible attachments can be opened or saved. (You'll get an error message if you try to open an attachment that is not a compatible file type.)

1. In any inbox, tap any email that contains an attachment.
2. Scroll to the bottom of the email.
3. If applicable, tap **Download Complete Message**. Embedded pictures will appear when you do.
4. Tap **Open** to view any attachment.
5. If prompted to choose what application to use, tap the desired option.
6. Tap the screen and tap the **Back** button to return to the message.

mainly be interested in saving pictures that are JPEGs; short videos that are MP4s; PDF files; and Microsoft Word, Excel, and PowerPoint documents.

Figure 7-6 shows an example of an email with an attachment that is an MP4 file. That's a video. Because it's a compatible file type, it can be downloaded, opened (played), and saved.

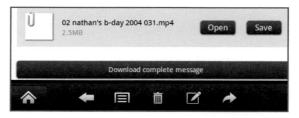

Figure 7-6: *After you tap Download Complete Message, you can play or save a compatible attached file.*

In this instance, the video will play in the Gallery app, and the saved file will be available from there as well, under the Download option, shown here. Pictures you open or save will appear in the Gallery too.

You'll find attachments you save in other areas of your Kindle Fire too, depending on the file type. For instance, if you save a Microsoft Word document, it will be saved to the Internal Storage Download folder. You access

CAUTION

Attachments you save aren't stored in the cloud; they are stored on your Kindle Fire. Remember, you only have about 6GB of storage space to work with, so be aware of how much you're saving.

that folder from Quickoffice, which you'll learn about in Chapter 9. PDF files are stored in a special area too, and you can easily view a list of saved PDFs from the Adobe Reader app. Because attachments vary so much, it's best to remember this:

- If you see the option Download Complete Message at the bottom of an email, tap it before attempting to play or view an attachment.
- After opening an attachment, tap the screen and then the Back button to close the attachment and return to the message.
- After saving an attachment, to open it again, think about what program or app you'd use to view it in the first place. Then, look for downloaded pictures and videos in the Gallery app, look for PDFs in the Adobe Reader app, and look for office documents in the Quickoffice app.
- You can transfer attachments you've saved to your Kindle Fire via USB to your computer. Once connected, to find the saved attachments, navigate to the Kindle Fire's Download folder. If you don't see what you want there, try the Documents folder.
- You can locate and play MP3 files you've saved from attachments if you open Quickoffice, navigate to Internal Storage, and tap the Download folder.
- You can save a .vcf file included as an email attachment and it will integrate the information with the Contacts and Email app automatically.

Mark an Email as Spam

Some of the email you receive is not email you wish to receive. You can report unwanted email, called spam, to your web-based email provider. You can't report spam to POP3 providers. To report spam:

1. Open the email.
2. Tap the **Menu** icon.
3. Tap **Mark As Spam**. The email will be deleted.

Compose and Respond to Email

The Email app is quite robust, and there was a lot to learn about accessing and reading email and working with attachments. With that out of the way, you can now discover how to compose new email and respond to what you receive.

Compose a New Email

To compose a new email, you must first access an inbox. This can be the Unified Inbox or the inbox for a specific email account you've configured. If you compose a new email from the Unified Inbox, the email account set as the default during setup will be used for sending. If you choose a specific account that is not set as the default account, email will be sent from that account instead. Figure 7-7 shows the Compose button you'll tap to start a new email, along with callouts for the Refresh button and others.

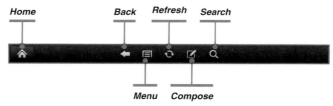

Figure 7-7: **The Email app, like others, has an Options bar with buttons on it.**

To compose a simple email:

1. In the Email app, tap any inbox.
2. Tap the **Compose** button.
3. Type an email address in the **To** line. If the contact appears while you're typing, you can tap it to enter it quickly. Repeat as desired, separating addresses with commas.
4. Tap **Next** on the keyboard or tap inside the **Subject** line.
5. Type a subject. See Figure 7-8.

> **NOTE**
>
> You can change the sending email address during composition if multiple email accounts are configured, no matter what inbox you use to compose it.

To — Joli Ballew <Joli_Ballew@hotmail.com>,   **Show CC and BCC fields** — Cc/Bcc

Subject — Lunch?

Choose a different sending account — Send as joli_ballew@tx.rr.com ▾   **Send** — Send

Attach a file — Attach   Send   Save Draft   Cancel — **Cancel**

Save for later — Save Draft

Hide the keyboard

Figure 7-8: *When you compose an email from scratch, you must enter the recipients, a subject, and a message.*

6. Note the **Send As** entry. If you have multiple accounts and want to send from a different one, tap this and select the desired account.

7. Tap **Next** and type the message body.

8. Tap the keyboard icon to hide the keyboard and review your work.

9. Tap **Send** when ready.

Save an Email and Complete It Later

If you start an email and decide you want to complete it and send it later, during composition, first make a note of the email account listed next to Send As. You'll need to know that information to find the draft later. When you are ready to save the email as a draft, tap **Save Draft**. That's the easy part, and you saw the Save Draft button in Figure 7-8. Finding that draft later when you're ready to edit and send takes a little more effort.

To locate a draft email you've saved:

1. In the Email app, tap the **Back** button as applicable to navigate to the main Accounts screen. You want to be on the screen that shows the Unified Inbox and any other configured account inboxes.

QUICKSTEPS

RESPONDING TO EMAIL

There are many ways to respond to an email. You can forward it, reply to all of the recipients of an email, or reply only to the sender. To reply to an email:

1. Open the email.

2. Tap the **Reply** button. It's the right-facing arrow.

3. Tap **Reply**, **Reply All**, or **Forward**.

Reply   Reply all   Forward

4. Complete the email as desired and tap **Send**.

NOTE

The folders you see when you tap Folders will vary depending on the type of email account you've selected (web-based, POP3, or IMAP), the folders preconfigured by the email provider, and the folders you've previously created yourself. All account types should have a Drafts folder though.

2. Tap the account you used to create the draft. This may be Gmail, Time Warner, Verizon, or AOL, for example.

3. Tap the **Menu** button and tap **Folders**.

4. Tap **Drafts**. See Figure 7-9. Here that's shown as [Gmail]/Drafts.

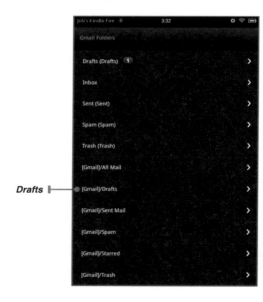

Drafts

Figure 7-9: **Drafts is always an option under Folders, but not all providers offer Spam, Starred, All Mail, and others you see here from Gmail.**

5. Tap the desired email to open it and complete as desired.

Include an Attachment in an Email

You already know how to open and save attachments you receive, but you may not yet have added an attachment to send with an outgoing email. You can add attachments while using the Email app to a new email or to email you are replying to or forwarding. Two applications come preinstalled on your Kindle Fire that can be used to attach something to an email you're composing: Gallery and Quickoffice. You may see other options as you acquire compatible apps. This is what you'll see when you tap Attach, with only the default applications in place.

If you aren't in the Email app but come across a picture or document you'd like to send to someone via email, instead of opening the Email app and attaching it, you can attach it from the current application. For instance, if you tap and hold a picture in the Gallery app and tap Share, you can then choose Send With Email. When you approach it this way, a new email opens with the item attached.

To attach a document from the Email app using Quickoffice:

1. Open the **Email** app.

2. Enter any inbox.

3. Tap the **Compose** button.

4. Compose your email as desired, and then tap **Attach**.

5. Tap **Quickoffice**.

6. Locate the file you want to attach. It will be under Internal Storage or Recent Documents.

7. Tap the file you want to attach.

8. Complete the email and tap **Send**.

To attach an image to a new email from inside the Gallery:

1. Open the Gallery app. (You can find it under the Apps tab under Device.)

2. Tap **Pictures**.

3. Tap and hold briefly on the first picture you want to attach. Tap additional pictures if necessary.

4. Tap **Share**.

5. Tap **Send With Email**.

6. Complete the email as desired and tap **Send**. See Figure 7-10.

ADDING CC AND BCC RECIPIENTS TO AN EMAIL

When you add recipients to the CC line of an email, it is understood that they need to read (and perhaps save) the email but not reply. All recipients can see who is in the CC line of an email. When you add recipients to the BCC line of an email, it is understood that they should read the email and that no other recipients know that they are included in it.

1. Tap **Compose** to begin a new email, or opt to reply to or forward an existing one.

2. Tap the **CC/BCC** icon to the right of the To line.

3. Tap in the new lines that appear to enter email addresses.

4. Complete the email as desired.

TIP

You can send an email from a contact card. To access the card, tap the contact name quickly.

Figure 7-10: *Attached files appear in the email under the Message text area; tap the X to remove any prior to sending.*

Start an Email from Your Contacts List

If you opted to import contacts when you set up your email accounts at the beginning of this chapter, you'll have some contacts available on your Kindle Fire. Specifically, you'll have the contacts you've previously associated with the email account you configured. You'll learn about the Contacts app in Chapter 9, but because you can start an email inside this app, it's worth noting in this chapter. To get started, return to the Home screen, then:

1. Tap **Apps**.
2. Tap **Contacts**.

3. Scroll to locate a contact you want to send an email to.
4. Tap and hold the contact name.

If you receive an address card in an email as an attachment and save that card to the Kindle Fire's internal storage, from the Contacts app, you can tap the **Menu** icon and tap **Import/Export** to add that card to your contacts list.

5. Tap **Send Email To**, shown in Figure 7-11.

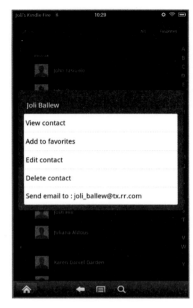

*Figure 7-11: **Tap and hold any contact to access these options.***

6. Complete the email as desired.

Add Recipients Using the Contacts List

If you opted to import contacts when you set up the email accounts on your Kindle Fire, and if you had contacts available, those contacts are stored and available in the Contacts app. Because the Contacts app and the Email app are integrated, you can select recipients from that list (and from the app) when composing emails. You may have already seen an example of the former while typing a name in the To line of an email. Figure 7-12 shows an example. If you see what you want in the options, you can tap to add it quickly.

Notice the orange + sign in Figure 7-12. If you tap that icon, your list of contacts (as stored in the Contacts app) becomes available. From there you can select a recipient easily by tapping the desired name. As noted earlier, you'll learn more about the Contacts app in Chapter 9; for now, it's only important that you know the two apps, Contacts and Email, are integrated and work together behind the scenes to make emailing easier.

Manage Email

To best manage email that arrives on your Kindle Fire, you must keep it from amassing. Your inboxes should only contain email you've yet to read, delete, save, or file. In addition, you should only receive email from accounts you use with your Kindle Fire. Just because you have five email accounts doesn't mean they all need to be active and retrieving mail on the device! So, the first step in managing your email is to learn how to minimize the email you receive, and the second is to learn how to quickly delete email you receive and do not need to keep.

Once that's done, you can create a filing system for email you can't get rid of immediately, like travel itineraries, class schedules, maps, and the like. Creating folders isn't a feature that's built into the Email app, but there's a workaround.

Delete Multiple Emails

You should delete email you don't want to keep as it arrives, so your inboxes don't get bogged down with email messages. When you delete an email from your Kindle Fire, by default, it is not deleted from other places, including but not limited to smart phones or tablets you use, computers, or the email provider's website. You'll still be able to access the email from there successfully. Thus, it's safe to delete email you receive on your Kindle Fire even if you still need to have access to it from other devices.

You already know how to delete a single email, and you can use that technique to delete messages one at a time. Using this method can become tiresome, however, if you have to delete more than a few. Thus, your Kindle Fire offers a way to delete multiple emails at one time.

1. Open the Email app and any inbox.
2. Tap the **Menu** icon.
3. Tap **Edit List**.
4. Tap the left side of every email you want to delete. A check mark will appear in each.
5. Tap **Delete** when finished.

TIP

To get rid of a web-based email for good, delete it at the provider's website. Alternatively, configure the settings on your Kindle Fire or another compatible device to delete the email from the server once you delete it there.

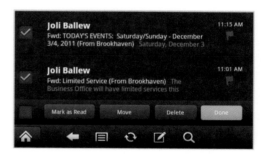

6. Repeat as desired, and then tap **Done**.

Remove an Email Account

If you decide after a period of time that you receive too many emails on your Kindle Fire, consider removing your configured email accounts and direct friends and family to use only one that you leave active on your Kindle. As an example, you can create a new Gmail account (perhaps JolisFriendsandFamily@ gmail.com), configure it on your home computer, smart phone, and Kindle Fire, and direct the most important people in your life to use that account when they want to email you. Then, configure only this account on your Kindle and remove the rest. This way you won't be burdened with spam (for a while anyway); emails from work; or emails from mailing lists, newsgroups, and similar entities.

If you'd like to remove an email account already configured on your Kindle Fire:

1. Open the Email app.
2. Navigate to the screen that shows all of your configured accounts and the Unified Inbox.
3. Tap and hold the account you want to remove.
4. Tap **Remove Account**.
5. Tap **OK**.

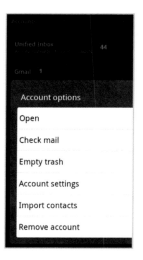

Create Folders with Gmail

You can't create folders in the Email app and move mail into them for posterity. However, if you use a Gmail account (or another web-based account that offers similar features), and you already had folders configured when you set up the account on your Kindle Fire, those folders will appear on your Kindle Fire. If that is the case, you can use those folders to manage the mail you want to keep by moving email out of your inbox and into those folders.

CAUTION

Right now, new folders you create at the Gmail website don't get synced to your Kindle Fire. This means that only folders that were created *before* you set up your Gmail account on your Kindle Fire will be available on it. You can create new folders and then force a sync of them by removing the Gmail account from your Kindle Fire and re-creating it.

To create folders for your web-based email account, visit the provider's website. Look for the option to create a folder, and follow the instructions to do so. Once you're finished, look for those folders to be synced to the corresponding account on your Kindle Fire. Figure 7-13 shows the options from Google's Gmail. If the new folders don't appear on your Kindle Fire after an hour or so, you'll have to force a sync. To do this, remove the account and re-create it. The newly created folders will appear.

Figure 7-13: *Gmail calls its folders "labels"; other providers use the term Folders.*

Move an Email into a Folder

If you have access to folders on your Kindle Fire from Gmail or another web-based email account, you can move an email that arrives through that account to the folder to file it there. To move an email to a folder:

1. Navigate to an email on your Kindle Fire that arrived through the web-based account.
2. Tap the email to open it.
3. Tap the **Menu** icon and tap **Move**.
4. Tap the desired folder in the list.

Explore Account Settings

There aren't any settings you need to be concerned about with regard to the Email app. There are only logging options, which won't likely apply to you. You may be interested in the settings available for your configured email accounts

CONSIDERING THIRD-PARTY EMAIL APPS

If you can't configure a specific email account, if forwarding your email to a compatible email address doesn't work for you, if folders you create for your web-based email accounts don't sync to the Kindle Fire as you'd expect, or if you've been unable to figure out how to manage the forwarded mail you've configured, consider downloading and installing a third-party email app from the Appstore. Search for "Email app for Fire." You'll see lots of email programs, including one from Yahoo! Mail.

though. With these options, you can change the default behavior of the account, including the sound that plays when new mail arrives, and you can create a signature for outgoing messages you compose on your Kindle Fire.

To access settings for an email account you've configured:

1. Open the Email app and navigate to any inbox *except* the Unified Inbox.
2. Tap the **Menu** icon and tap **Settings**.
3. Review all of the available settings.
4. To make any changes, tap the setting you want to change. Figure 7-14 shows the options for a POP3 account. A few you may want to change include:

Figure 7-14: **Tap any option here to change the settings for it.**

a. **Notification Sound** The sound that plays when new mail arrives.

b. **Fetch New Messages** To configure how often the Email app should check for messages, if ever.

c. **Default Account** To state which email account to use as the default for sending email if more than one account is configured.

d. Account Name   To change the name of the account as it appears in the Email app.

e. Composition Defaults   To create and add a signature, among other things.

f. When I Delete A Message   To change the default setting of Do Not Delete On Server, to delete the message from the server too, or to mark it as read on the server.

5. Tap the desired setting from the results. Here, the options for Fetch New Messages are shown.

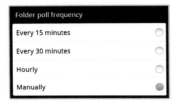

6. Explore additional settings as time allows.

There are plenty of settings to explore, but you don't have to. You can leave the defaults as they are and only explore the options. If you ever decide to make a change, you know where to go!

Chapter 8

Surfing the Web with Amazon Silk

A web browser lets you surf the Internet. You're already familiar with browsers; you probably use Internet Explorer on a PC or Safari on a Mac, for instance, to navigate the Internet. The Kindle Fire has a browser, too, and it is called Amazon Silk.

Many of the features you're used to already are available in Amazon Silk. You can surf the Web by typing in addresses or performing searches; create and save bookmarks; have multiple webpages open at once; and you can view pictures, videos, and similar media easily. Amazon Silk maintains a history of websites you've visited, can be configured to remember passwords, and provides access to lots of settings for personalizing it. In this chapter, you'll learn how to use Amazon Silk and how to take advantage of all its features.

8

Surf the Web

As you know, you'll need to be in range of and connected to a Wi-Fi network to access the Internet. The Kindle Fire doesn't offer a 3G plan for accessing the Internet when you're away from such a network. When you're connected, surfing the Web is fast and simple.

The first time you open Amazon Silk you'll see a list of prepopulated bookmarks. These bookmarks will change to reflect the sites you visit most. Here, you can see a sample; these bookmarks are already changed from the defaults, but do include several you'll see on your own Kindle Fire. Tap any bookmark to get started.

1
2
3
4
5
6
7
8
9
10

TIP

Note the similarities between Amazon Silk and other web browsers you've used, namely the Back and Forward buttons and the ability to type a specific web address in the Location bar (or search from it).

Navigate to Webpages

Amazon Silk is a powerful web browser and offers lots of features. Figure 8-1 shows the interface. As with other applications, you move around in the browser by tapping and flicking. (If, instead of a webpage, you see a group of icons, tap the one for Amazon to access what's shown here.)

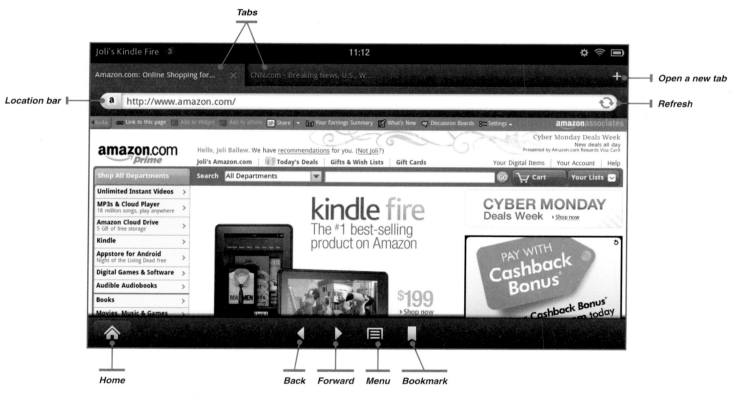

Tabs

Open a new tab

Location bar

Refresh

Home   Back   Forward   Menu   Bookmark

Figure 8-1: Amazon Silk has quite a few features, many of which you are already likely familiar with.

TIP

If you'd rather search from www.google.com, type that in the Search bar and then type your keywords into Google's Search window.

As with other web browsers you've used, you can search for something specific from any webpage.

1. With any webpage open, tap the Location bar. If you don't see this, flick to scroll to the top of the page.

2. Type a few keywords.

3. Although you can tap a result that appears under your keywords, as shown in Figure 8-2, it's often best to simply tap **Go** on the keyboard.

Figure 8-2: *Tap Go to show Google results for your search words.*

4. Tap an item in the search results to go to the desired page.

You can also type a web address, called a URL (Uniform Resource Locator), into the Location bar to navigate to that page directly.

1. Tap the Location bar.

2. On the keyboard that appears, type the website's address. If it starts with "http://www", you don't have to type that.

3. Tap **Go**.

It's important to notice when you visit a site that you may be automatically directed to the "mobile" version of it. For instance, Figure 8-3 shows the mobile version of Yahoo.com. It's easy to scroll through the page and access what's available, and mobile versions of pages are quite popular among tablet users. One way to determine that the website you're visiting is the mobile version is to look for the "m" just after the "http://" in the Location bar.

Figure 8-3: *Mobile versions of sites look better on smaller screens but generally don't offer the features the desktop versions do.*

You won't always want to access the mobile site, though. If you need to access features unavailable on the mobile version, you'll want to switch to the desktop version. You can almost always do that at the bottom of a mobile webpage. As shown here, you can tap Desktop to make the switch.

Notice how much different the desktop version of the Yahoo! page looks from its mobile counterpart. Figure 8-4 shows this. Notice how the links on the left are small; you'd have to zoom in to access those effectively. Also notice that you have access to all of the Yahoo! features, including the option to sign in, get mail, and search the Web in various ways (Web, Images, Video, Local, Apps, and More).

USING SOCIAL NETWORKING SITES

If you visit a social networking site like Facebook, Twitter, LinkedIn, or MySpace on your Kindle Fire, you'll be redirected to the mobile version of the page. It won't look like what you're used to seeing on your computer, and it won't offer all of the same features (and it may be difficult to find the option to view the page in its desktop version). You have two options if you do not like the mobile view: You can search for an app in the Appstore to use instead, or you can tell your Kindle Fire you want it to always open websites optimized for desktop view. Desktop view is awfully small, though, as shown here for Facebook.

Figure 8-4: **The desktop version of a page is harder to navigate because it is not enhanced for mobile, but instead enhanced for computer screens; but all of the elements you're used to are there.**

Explore Gestures

Your Kindle Fire enables you to use "gestures" to perform tasks. You've used gestures already, including tapping the screen to select an item or flicking to toss an angry bird at a group of pigs. Gestures are available for Amazon Silk too.

Try these gestures with a webpage open (and note you'll learn more about many of these features in this chapter):

- Pinch in or out to zoom in or out on a webpage.
- Swipe or flick left or right to see content that cannot be viewed on a webpage (especially those you've zoomed in on).
- Swipe or flick up and down to see content that cannot be viewed on a webpage (or those you've zoomed in on). Most pages offer information that runs more than one full screen.

1 2 3 4 5 6 7 8 9 10

If you need to find a word on a page, tap the **Menu** icon on the Options bar, tap **Find In Page**, and type the word you're looking for. You'll learn more about the Menu icon throughout this chapter.

- Tap the + sign to access the available bookmarks; tap any "tile" to access that webpage.

- Tap the X shown on any tab to close that tab.
- Tap and hold any link to view the option to open it in a new tab.
- Tap and hold any link to bookmark it, copy it, or share it with others.
- Tap and hold any bookmark tile to delete it, share it, and more.

Open a Webpage in a New Tab

You can have more than one webpage available at a time. You do this with tabbed browsing. Figure 8-5 shows Amazon Silk with several tabs open. To access a site represented by a tab, simply click the tab title.

There are various ways to use tabs when surfing the Web:

- You can open a new tab and navigate to a page you've bookmarked or one that has been prepopulated. (Tap + and tap a tile.)
- You can open a new, blank tab and use it to navigate to a webpage by searching or typing a URL in the Location bar. (Tap + and type in the Location bar.)
- You can open a link on an existing page in its own tab, so both the source page and the linked page will be available. (Tap and hold any link, and choose the desired option from the results.)

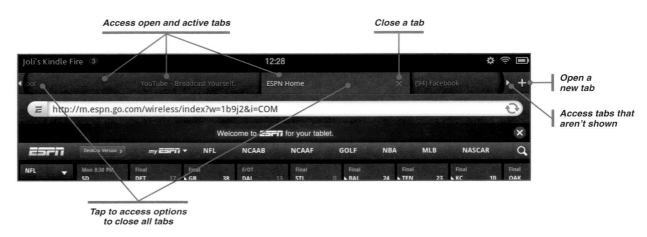

Access open and active tabs

Close a tab

Open a new tab

Access tabs that aren't shown

Tap to access options to close all tabs

Figure 8-5: **Tabs enable you to have multiple webpages available at the same time.**

> **NOTE**
>
> If you notice the information on a webpage is outdated, even if by only a couple of minutes, tap the **Refresh** button to reload the page.

> **NOTE**
>
> Tap **Save Link** when you want to download something and save it to your Kindle Fire. The practical use for this is to tap Save Link for a URL embedded in a webpage. When you do, you'll see a notification on the status bar. When the "download" is finished, you'll see a number there. Tap the number to access the link.

- You can close all tabs by tapping and holding a tab title and selecting Close Tab, Close Other Tabs, or Close All Tabs. (Tap to the right of any tab name, and then tap the desired option from the resulting list.)
- You can access tabs that can't be viewed by flicking left and right. (Tap and drag any tab to the left or right.)

To open a new tab and navigate to a webpage:

1. Tap the + sign.
2. To navigate to a bookmarked page, tap the tile that represents it.
3. To navigate to a URL, type the URL in the Location bar.
4. To search using keywords, tap the Location bar and type the desired words, and then tap **Go** on the keyboard.

To open a link in its own tab:

1. While at a webpage, locate a link to another page.
2. Tap and hold the link.
3. Tap the desired choice; in this case, **Open In New Tab**.

Open

Open in new tab

Bookmark link

Save link

Copy link URL

Share link

COPYING AND PASTING URLS

You can copy a URL in two ways: You can tap and hold the address in the Location bar, or you can tap and hold a link that appears on a webpage. Both methods offer a Copy option. Once you've copied the URL, tap and hold in any compatible app to paste it.

1. Tap and hold a web address in the Location bar.

2. Tap **Copy** or **Copy Link URL**.

3. Open any compatible app, tap and hold where text can be input, and tap **Paste**.

Edit text
Paste
Input method

TIP

The difference between the options Open and Open In New Tab is that when you tap Open, the current page is replaced with the page represented by the link. If you tap Open In New Tab, the link opens in a new tab and leaves the current page open and available on its own.

Explore Additional Tap and Hold Options

There are a few additional things you can do after tapping and holding a screen element that haven't yet been covered here. Some of these options involve bookmarking websites, which you'll learn about shortly; others offer the ability to save something associated with a link and various options for sharing those links. What you see as options depends on what kind of screen element you tap and hold. As you can see in Figure 8-6, when you tap and hold a JPEG image, you have the option to save that image, among other things.

Figure 8-6: **Tap Save Image on a JPEG file to download the image to your Kindle Fire's internal storage; you can access saved JPEGs later from the Gallery.**

Another common option you'll see in many of the tap and hold option boxes is one that enables you to share the link. When you choose one of these share options, a new dialog box appears. What you see depends on what you have installed on your Kindle Fire. You can always send the link in an email (using the Email app), and if you've installed and configured additional apps like Facebook or a Notes app, you can use those instead.

You may not want to share a link to a URL, because what you want to share is a quote on the page, a sports stat, a recipe, or some other text. In these cases, it's often best to select just the text to share, copy it, and paste it in an email or note. What you see after you select text and then tap it to copy it depends on where you select the text from. For instance, if you type your user name in a log-in window and then select the text to copy it, you see a pop-up options box where you must make the choice to copy. If you copy text from a webpage and tap that text, you will likely only see a small note that says "Text Copied to Clipboard." Because of this, go ahead and work through the steps here to copy text on a webpage, and then tap it to see your options.

To select text to copy:

1. Tap and hold some text on a webpage.

2. Drag from the sliders that appear to select the desired text. If sliders do not appear, something else should, like an options box that lets you select either a word or everything on the page. Whatever you choose, the sliders you see here will become available.

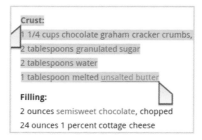

3. Tap or tap and hold the selected text to review your options.

4. If you see Copy, you can copy the text and paste it later. If you see Text Copied To Clipboard, it's available to paste as well.

5. If you want to paste the copied text, do so before you copy something else!

View and Control Flash Media

Adobe created a product called Adobe Flash a long time ago. This software is responsible for enabling the delivery of quite a bit of the media available on the Web to computers and mobile devices. Much of this media consists of videos and computer animations. Not all mobile devices are "Flash-compatible," but your Kindle Fire is. This means that you can view Flash media on your Kindle seamlessly.

Several familiar entities use Flash to deliver content, including but not limited to:

- YouTube
- Netflix
- CNN and related news sites
- Hulu

To experience Flash media, visit www.YouTube.com and search through the videos. Once you've selected a video to play, you can control it with video controls similar to what you learned about in Chapter 5.

To view web-based video on your Kindle Fire:

1. In Amazon Silk, tap the **+** sign.
2. Tap the bookmark for YouTube. (If you've deleted it, you'll have to type YouTube .com in the Location bar.)
3. Navigate to any video you want to play. Note that you can search for videos.
4. Tap the icon for the video and wait for the video to load (you may have to watch an ad before the video plays).

TIP

If an ad appears over the video, tap the X that appears with it to hide the ad.

5. To control the media playback:

    a. Scroll if necessary so you can view the controls. The controls are shown in Figure 8-7.

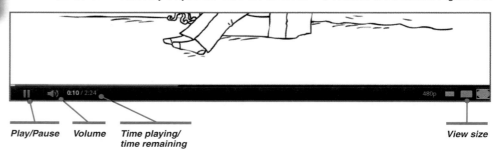

Play/Pause   Volume   Time playing/   View size
                               time remaining

Figure 8-7: **Video controls help you manage video playback.**

TIP

To access a page you've visited recently but did or did not bookmark, tap the **Menu** icon and tap **History**. Then you can tap any item in the list to open the page.

    b. Tap the **Pause** button to stop the video. Tap **Play** to restart it. (You can also tap the video itself.)

    c. Tap the **Volume** icon to change the volume.

    d. Tap the screen size buttons to change the viewing size.

Create and Manage Bookmarks

By now you've explored your Kindle Fire's prepopulated bookmarks. The bookmark icons are called "tiles," and you can touch any one of them to go to the bookmarked site. These prepopulated bookmarks are smart too; they'll change to represent the sites you visit most over a period of time as Amazon Silk learns your preferences. More bookmark features are available, including the ability to create your own bookmarks and give them personalized names. You can also delete bookmarks you no longer want, share bookmarks, and copy their URLs.

Add a Bookmark

It's easy to add a bookmark. Just navigate to the page to bookmark and then:

1. Tap the **Menu** icon on the Options bar.

2. Tap **Add Bookmark**.

3. Either accept the name or type a new one.

4. Tap **OK**.

Open, Copy, Share, and Delete Bookmarks

You can easily manage the bookmarks you keep. To access the options, navigate to the screen that offers the bookmark tiles, and then tap and hold any tile to manage that particular bookmark.

To access a bookmark you've previously set and to open or delete it:

1. Tap the **+** sign at the top of the Amazon Silk browser. You can also tap the bookmark icon on the Options bar.

2. Tap and hold the bookmark tile you want to manage.

3. Tap **Open**, **Open In New Tab**, or **Delete** as desired. See Figure 8-8.

To copy and/or share a bookmark:

1. Tap the **+** sign at the top of the Amazon Silk browser.

2. Tap and hold the bookmark tile you want to manage.

3. Tap **Share Link** to select an application to share with (like Email), or tap **Copy Link URL** to copy the link to paste it later.

Joli Ballew

Open the bookmark in the currently opened tab ──● Open

●── Open the bookmark in a new tab
Open in new tab ●

Open the bookmark but do not navigate to the tab ──● Open in background tab

Share link ●── Share the link in an email, on Facebook, or using another compatible app

Copy the URL so you can paste it later ──● Copy link URL

Delete ●── Delete the bookmark

Figure 8-8: **You have six options for managing your bookmarks.**

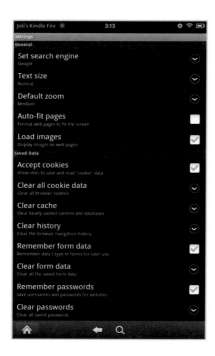

Configure Preferences and Settings

Some settings associated with Amazon Silk enable you to personalize the browser to suit your needs. As you might guess, you access these settings from the Options bar. Tap the **Menu** icon and tap **Settings** to view them. The Menu icon and the Settings option were both shown earlier in Figure 8-1. The Settings page is shown here.

Once you've accessed the settings, there are many areas to change. You can tap and review these options as time allows, but for now, here is a brief summary of a few of the options you may want to change right away. Following this list you'll learn how to make changes to a few others. You can then use this knowledge to personalize Amazon Silk as desired.

From the Amazon Silk's Settings options, you can

● Change the search engine from Google to Bing or Yahoo!

● Change the default text size of Normal to Tiny, Small, Large, or Huge

● Change the default zoom from Medium to Far or Close

- Opt not to load images on webpages

- Opt not to remember data for forms, such as your address and phone number

- Opt not to remember passwords

- Opt to open new tabs in the background and not make them immediately active

- Restore Amazon Silk settings to their defaults

Change the Default Webpage View

You have probably explored both mobile view and desktop view for the websites you visit most. You can configure settings for Amazon Silk so that either desktop view or mobile view is always used, or you can optimize the view for each website individually.

To change the default view for webpages you open in Amazon silk, perhaps to make all pages open in desktop view:

1. From the Options bar, tap **Settings**.

2. Scroll down to **Desktop Or Mobile View**.

3. Tap the arrow on the right side.

4. Make the appropriate choice.

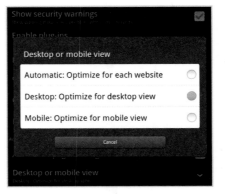

ACCESSING AND CONFIGURING SILK SETTINGS

To access the Amazon Silk Settings page:

1. From the Options bar, tap **Settings**.

2. Scroll to the desired option, and then:

   a. If the option has a check box beside it, tap to add or remove the check mark to enable or disable the setting, respectively.

   b. If the option has an arrow beside it, tap the arrow to view the options, and then make a choice.

Clear Browsing History and Cache

Your browsing history is a list of all of the websites you've visited recently. You can sort the list by sites you've visited this day, during the last seven days, or in the last month. This list can often be helpful when you need to return to a site you visited but did not bookmark. It can also be useful if you'd like to find out what websites others who have used your Kindle Fire have visited while using it. To access the list, tap the **Menu** icon and tap **History**. You can clear the list from the History list, shown here, or from Settings from the Clear History option.

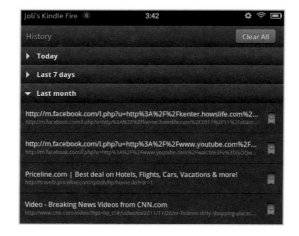

If you opt to clear your history from Settings:

1. Tap the **Menu** icon on the Options bar.

2. Tap **Settings**.

3. Scroll to locate **Clear History**.

4. Tap the arrow beside it.

5. Tap **OK**.

Cache is information stored on your Kindle Fire to help you browse the Web faster. It works like this: When you visit a website, everything on the webpage must load onto your Kindle Fire. Some of that information never changes, like the logo, the information that appears at the bottom of the page, and even some pictures. To keep from having to download this same information every time you visit the page, some of it is saved into "cache." Then, when you want to load the page again, Amazon Silk can pull what's in cache faster than it can pull it from the Web. This makes for a faster web experience.

You should clear your browser's cache if you are having problems loading webpages or you think the data being loaded is outdated.

To clear your cache:

1. Tap the **Menu** icon on the Options bar.
2. Scroll down and tap the arrow by **Clear Cache**.
3. Tap **OK**.

How to...

Chapter 9
Using the Kindle Fire at Home, for Business, and for Travel

You can use your Kindle Fire at home, at work, and while you travel. You can use it to make purchases from Amazon.com, get apps for almost any imaginable business purpose, view Really Simple Syndication (RSS) feeds that pertain to your work or hobbies, upload and open personal documents, and more. You can even purchase accessories for when you travel, connect to personal hotspots you create with other mobile devices, and use your Kindle Fire on a plane.

Shop at Amazon.com

So far, you've shopped at Amazon for a lot of things, namely books, music, apps, and movies, likely all of which you've opted to have delivered wirelessly to your Kindle Fire or your computer. You can shop at Amazon for physical

TIP

Amazon offers their own apps, and one is called Amazon Santa. This app lets kids and parents create personalized holiday wish lists to share with others. It's a great way to keep track of items you'd like to purchase through an app. Keep your eyes open for similar apps in the future.

NOTE

Amazon offers subscription services you can set up so that you'll receive what you need on a schedule. For instance, you can create a subscription to have Amazon send you a new filter for your refrigerator every nine months, a ream of paper for your business once a month, or even flowers for your wife each year on your anniversary. You can cancel any subscription at any time, or create new ones at no charge.

things, too, including household items and business supplies, games and toys, pet supplies, and more, and you can have those items delivered to your home or place of business easily. You can even shop for gifts and have those delivered to a recipient of your choice at their own mailing address.

If you have an urge to immediately dismiss online shopping because of the associated shipping costs, note that these costs can be minimized or eliminated. If you are an Amazon Prime member and choose from any of the thousands of eligible products, you can get free two-day shipping on the items you buy. If you are not an Amazon Prime member and opt for any of the thousands of "free super saver shipping" items, you can still avoid shipping costs, although it will take around a week for purchases to arrive and you'll have to spend a specific amount of money (currently $25). Amazon also offers free shipping under other circumstances; for instance, new moms and dads can sign up for monthly diaper delivery and forgo shipping on those products and related ones. Similar programs exist that can be explored. Figure 9-1 shows the option to sort results by what's Prime Eligible.

Sort by Prime Eligible

Figure 9-1: **To minimize shipping costs, select items that qualify for free "super saver" shipping.**

Order Products for Your Home

Think about all of the items you make special trips to special stores for. Perhaps you buy art supplies from an art store, pet supplies from a pet store, and printer supplies from a computer store. Of course, you buy a lot of mundane things, too, including toothpaste and toilet paper. If you know the prices you pay for these items, you can compare them to what you'd have to pay at Amazon.com for the same things. If the price is competitive, and if you can get free shipping, it might be worth your while to learn how to make these purchases online, versus driving all over town to acquire them.

To order physical items from Amazon using your Kindle Fire:

1. From the Home screen, tap **Web**.
2. Tap the **+** sign.
3. Either tap the bookmark for Amazon.com or type Amazon.com into the Location bar and tap **Go**.

4. Use any navigation techniques you know to locate the item you want to buy.
5. Tap **Add To Cart**.
6. Continue shopping as desired. When you're ready to check out, tap **Cart** near the top of any Amazon page or tap **Proceed To Checkout**.
7. Type your password and tap **Sign In Using Our Secure Server**.
8. If applicable, input a new shipping address; select the address and tap **Ship To This Address**.
9. Note your personalized shipping options. Select one.

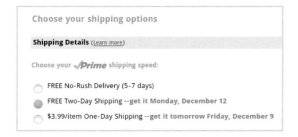

NOTE

As with other Amazon purchases, you'll receive a confirmation email.

NOTE

You may need to use a different credit card or account when shopping for business-related supplies.

QUICKFACTS

USING TWO AMAZON ACCOUNTS

You may prefer or be required to use a specific credit card or a separate business account when shopping at Amazon. It's easy to choose a different credit card during the checkout process, but if you're required to use a different Amazon account, you'll have to log out of Amazon with your personal account and log back in with the account you need to make purchases with. To log out of one Amazon account and log in with another:

1. From the Home screen, tap **Web**.

2. Navigate to Amazon.com.

3. At the top of the page, note the option that says **Not**, followed by your name and a question mark. Tap your name.

4. Type your business account information and tap **Sign In Using Our Secure Server**.

Hello, Joli Ballew. We have recommendations for you. (Not Joli?)

10. Scroll down, if necessary, and tap **Continue**.

11. Select your method of payment or enter a new payment method. Tap **Continue**.

12. Review your order, making any changes as applicable, and tap **Continue**.

13. Tap **Place Your Order**.

Order Products for Your Business

Just as you regularly purchase items for your home, you may also purchase items for your business. These items may include copy paper, printer toner, paper clips, thumbtacks, and similar items. If the price is competitive, it may be worth your while to have those items delivered from Amazon. As with home purchases, compare prices first. Then consider what you currently spend in gas or delivery charges, and how much of your time you use acquiring these items. If you can come out ahead with Amazon, consider making the switch.

Discover Useful Business Apps

If you use your Kindle Fire for business, you'll want to have access to the most useful business apps available. The most popular apps vary over time, but there are some tried and true apps that are must-haves and are always available from the Top Apps list in the Appstore. In addition to what's available from the Appstore, you can incorporate various free cloud applications from Google. These aren't apps as you know them; these are web-based applications you can access, use, and update from any Internet-enabled device.

Search the Appstore for Top Business Apps

The Appstore offers apps for just about any task imaginable. For example, you may need an RSS reader to keep up with your favorite feeds, or an app that can follow stock prices. You'll probably need an app that lets you open and edit word processing files. If you think outside the box, you may be able to use an app that can locate the nearest five-star restaurant when you need to impress a client, or an app that can locate the nearest printer store, computer store, or office supply chain.

TIP

If you need to create, access, edit, and share Microsoft Word documents, Excel spreadsheets, and PowerPoint presentations from your Kindle Fire, get Quickoffice Pro, OfficeSuite Pro 5, Documents to Go Full Version, or a similar app.

TIP

Always read app reviews before buying an app.

To find the most popular, and hopefully useful, business apps:

1. From the Home screen, tap **Apps**.

2. Tap **Store**.

3. Scroll right and tap **All Categories**.

4. Tap the category that applies to your specific needs. Try **City Info**, **Communication**, **Education**, **Finance**, **Navigation**, or **Productivity**, for starters.

5. In the resulting list, tap **Top** (see Figure 9-2).

Figure 9-2: The apps listed under Top are the bestselling and most popular.

6. Tap any app to learn more about it and read the reviews.

Many apps from the Appstore can come in quite handy, especially apps that let you open and view (and maybe even edit) specific file types you'd otherwise be unable to work with on your Kindle Fire. Apps that let you check stock prices or

VIEWING RSS FEEDS

RSS stands for Really Simple Syndication. It is a technology used to make newly changed data (like news or weather) more easily available to readers. It's a "feed," which means it changes often. You can subscribe to and access RSS feeds from Amazon Silk, or you can obtain and use an RSS reader from the Appstore. Since some RSS feeds have yet to be optimized for the Kindle Fire, an app is probably best for now. gReader is Google's RSS reader, it's free, and you can use it to read RSS feeds you choose. However, there are many other RSS reading apps, and it'll be your call regarding the one you acquire.

1. From the Home screen, tap **Apps**, and then tap **Store**.

2. In the Search box, tap **RSS**.

3. Obtain an RSS reader from the Appstore. Consider gReader.

4. Log in as required.

5. Tap the **+** sign (or perform a similar task) to add new feeds. You should see a list of feeds to choose from and an option to locate more by interest.

6. Locate the feeds you want to subscribe to and add them. Like any app, it'll take a little time to learn to use all of the features.

7. To read any feed, tap it in the feed list. Depending on the app, you may be able to share the story, translate it into another language, or mark it as a favorite, among other things.

find a five-star restaurant while on the go are also useful. Some apps, however, especially calendar apps, may not always be the best option when it comes to business. That's because you'll probably need to access the data you input into that app using your Kindle Fire on other mobile devices and computers. If there's no way to sync what you input into your Kindle Fire with a desktop computer or smartphone, you'll only have to input the information again on those devices. This will make managing your data more difficult. The same holds true for documents you open and edit on multiple devices. It's pretty easy to run into version control issues when you edit from more than one device. When you need to access data from multiple devices, you need to use a "cloud" application or service.

Explore Cloud Applications from Google

Applications that store data in the cloud are perfect if you access data on multiple devices. When data is stored in the cloud, any changes to the information (such as the addition of a new appointment or edits to a Word file) become available instantly at all of your other Internet-enabled computers, tablets, and smartphones. Google offers many free cloud applications you should consider. One is Calendar; another is Google Docs. Let's discuss Calendar first.

It is probably easier initially to set up your Google Calendar from a computer, although you can do it from your Kindle Fire. Once you've set it up, you can input data from anywhere, and access that data from anywhere too.

To get started with Google Calendar:

1. Using a web browser, navigate to www.google.com/calendar.

2. If applicable, create a Google account and/or log in.

3. Note the views and select one. Figure 9-3 shows Month.

4. To enter a new appointment, click any date or time. A window appears where you can input the desired information, shown in Figure 9-3.

5. Once you've input information, you can click to edit it.

6. You can now access your calendar when connected to the Internet from any device by navigating to www.google.com/calendar.

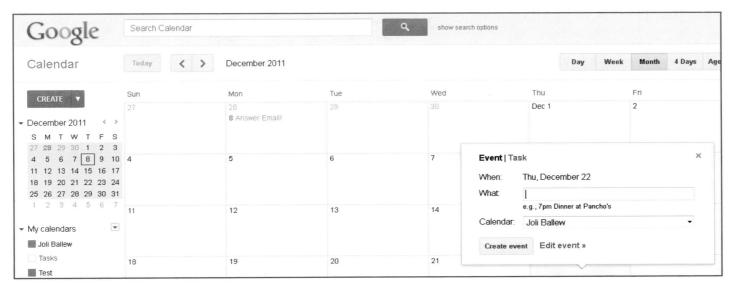

*Figure 9-3: **Google Calendar is a web-based application and works with devices that can access the Internet via a web browser.***

While you're at Google.com, explore other apps. Try Books, Blogs, Reader, and Documents, for starters. You'll learn a little about Google Docs later in this chapter.

Store Personal Documents in Your Cloud Drive

You know a lot about the cloud if you've read this book from the beginning. You know that the media you purchase from Amazon is stored in the cloud at no additional cost to you. You know that you also have 5GB of free space for your own personal data too. You can use that space to store music, among other things. And if you use up your designated free space, you can rent more. You learned in Chapter 4 that you can store more than music in the cloud, however. In fact, you can store your personal documents there, among other things. As with anything stored in the cloud, you can access what's been uploaded from any Internet-connected device.

In this section you'll learn how to store documents in the cloud so that you can access them from your Kindle Fire when you're on vacation or away on business. You may want to store business contracts, contact lists, wills and power of attorneys, a list of passwords for websites you access, and even maps or travel documents, like itineraries. However, just because you can store documents on Your Cloud Drive at Amazon doesn't mean you can open everything you store there on your Kindle Fire. You may need to acquire apps to help you in that regard.

Figure 9-4 shows the default folders that are already created in your area of Amazon's cloud, which are available now for uploading data. Note the option to upload files. You will upload files from your computer.

Figure 9-4: *Your Cloud Drive offers folders you can use to store all kinds of data, including documents.*

Recognize Compatible Cloud File Types

Figure 9-4 shows a personal Amazon cloud space with the four default folders: Documents, Pictures, Music, and Videos. You can create your own folders to hold data that doesn't fit in any of these. For instance, you can create a folder called Travel and upload all of your travel documents there. You could also

UPLOADING PERSONAL DOCUMENTS

You have to upload data from your computer to the cloud if you want to store it there. You can't upload personal data from your Kindle Fire. The computer you choose will likely be a PC or a Mac, but other compatible devices exist. On most devices, the process is as follows:

1. Open your Web browser.

2. Navigate to www.amazon.com and login.

3. Click **Your Digital Items**, and then click **Your Cloud Drive Files**.

4. Select any folder in the list.

5. Click **Upload Files**.

6. Click **Select Files to Upload**.

7. Browse to the file, select it, and click **Open** or another appropriate option.

Select a Cloud Drive destination folder for your files:

Step 1 [Travel ▾]

Step 2 **Select files to upload...**

File upload size is limited to 2 GB per file

CAUTION

Some files are quite large and can fill your 5GB of cloud space quickly. For the most part, video files and large PDF files fall into this category.

create a folder named Study Aids that contains flash cards, technical papers, and quizzes. You can create a folder named Business and upload Microsoft PowerPoint presentations and Excel spreadsheets. While you may not be able to access and read every item stored in those folders on your Kindle Fire, they will be accessible from other devices. Alternatively, you may be able to acquire apps that let you open and view incompatible file types not currently supported on your Kindle Fire.

To create a folder on Your Cloud Drive (this is easiest from a computer):

1. From any web browser, visit www.amazon.com and log in.

2. Tap or click **Your Digital Items**.

3. Tap or click **Your Cloud Drive Files**.

4. Tap or click **New Folder**.

5. Type a name for the new folder.

6. Tap or click **Save Folder**.

7. Repeat as desired. Figure 9-5 shows a folder named Travel that was recently created and a folder named PersonalDocs in the process of being created.

Figure 9-5: Create your own folders first, and then, from a computer, upload files to it.

Once you've created folders in Your Cloud Drive, you can start uploading files there. This list outlines the types of files you can open on your Kindle Fire,

although you can upload almost any type of file to Your Amazon Cloud Drive. You've seen some of this before in this book, but here's a comprehensive list for reference:

- **Documents**   AZW, AZW1, TXT, MOBI (unprotected), PRC, DOC. You may have TXT and DOC files on your computer; these are common word document formats. If you have Adobe Reader, you can also open PDF files. Likewise, with Quickoffice you can open and view Microsoft Word documents, Excel spreadsheets, and PowerPoint presentations.

- **Audio supported within music**   AAC LC/LTP, HE-AACv1 (AAC+), HE-AACv2 (enhanced AAC+), AMR-NB (.3gp), AMR-WB (.3gp), MP3, MIDI, Ogg Vorbis (.ogg), PCM/WAVE (.wav). You may have AAC and MP3 files on your computer; these are common music file types.

- **Images**   JPEG, PNG, GIF, BMP. You likely have all of these kinds of files on your computer, although most digital cameras store files as JPEGs, so your pictures will probably be in that format.

- **Video**   H.263 (.3gp, .mp4), H264 AVC (.3gp, .mp4), MPEG 4 SP/ASP (.3gp), VP8 (.webm). You may have .mp4 or MPEG 4 files on your computer; these are common video file types.

Access and View Personal Documents

Just about any piece of data you can upload to Your Cloud Drive can be accessed from any computer with a web browser, as well as from thousands of other compatible devices, provided the proper applications are installed. You can also access files that are compatible with your Kindle Fire from your Kindle Fire (see the earlier list of compatible file types). With the appropriate apps, you can view file types that aren't natively supported and often even edit those files as well.

How you choose to access the files you've stored in the cloud from other computers and devices is up to you. The process is different depending on the device. To access and view compatible files stored on Your Cloud Drive from your Amazon Kindle:

1. From the Home screen, tap **Web**.
2. Navigate to Amazon.com and tap **Your Digital Items**.

EXPLORING GOOGLE DOCS

Many types of files aren't natively supported on your Kindle Fire. To view those files, you'll have to acquire the appropriate apps. There is another way to view incompatible files though; you can upload them to Google Docs from your computer, and then access them from Google Docs inside the Amazon Silk web browser. In many cases you can edit those files too.

UPLOAD FILES TO DOCS.GOOGLE.COM FROM A COMPUTER

To get started, from your computer, upload some personal files to Docs.Google.com. You'll have to sign in with a Google account to get started. Once the files are uploaded, you can see them in a list, as shown here. (The icon to the right of Create is the Upload button.)

Continued . . .

3. Tap **Your Cloud Drive Files**.

4. Tap the desired folder.

5. Tap the desired file.

6. Wait while the file downloads; you can watch the status of the download from the status bar.

7. Tap the notification that appears on the status bar, and tap the desired download. See Figure 9-6.

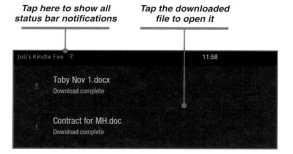

Figure 9-6: **The status bar offers access to the downloaded file.**

Use the Docs Tab

If you haven't explored the Docs tab, available from the Home screen, tap it now. There's not a lot to see except for the Kindle Fire User's guide. However, when you tap this tab, you'll see an email address you can use to send documents to your Kindle Fire. If you'd like to, you can send an email to this address from any computer or mobile device. Once it's received on your Kindle Fire, you can tap the item to open it. You can find the same documents and more from Quickoffice though, and Quickoffice is a much more robust application.

QUICKFACTS

EXPLORING GOOGLE DOCS (Continued)

ACCESS FILES FROM DOCS.GOOGLE.COM FROM YOUR KINDLE FIRE

Now, visit Docs.Google.Com from Amazon Silk on your Kindle Fire and log in. Browse to any file you've uploaded and open it inside the browser. You can now view, edit, and even play files that aren't currently compatible on your Kindle Fire. In addition, files accessed can often be edited.

Use Quickoffice and Adobe Reader

When you open a file stored in the cloud in the web browser, such as is the case with Google Docs, you don't have to worry about having an app to assist you. The capability is built into the web-based application and the app opens there. The same is true when you opt to play a Prime Instant Video at Amazon; playing the video is built right into the application itself. However, if you download data to your Kindle Fire from Your Cloud Files at Amazon, transfer data to your Kindle Fire via USB, or receive data in an email, you will need an app to open it.

The Kindle Fire comes with its own apps for this purpose. For instance, you use Gallery to view photos you save to your Kindle Fire. Quickoffice is another app that comes built in, and this app can be used to locate and open Microsoft Word documents, Excel spreadsheets, and PowerPoint presentations stored on your Kindle Fire (among other things). You may have other apps as well, like Adobe Reader for opening PDF files or Documents to Go to open other office file formats. Whatever the case, when you tap to open a compatible file, one of several things can happen:

- The app will open in the web-based application you used to retrieve it.
- The file will open in the Kindle Fire app you used to locate it.
- An app on your Kindle Fire will open with a prompt and you'll have to agree to terms of service and/or register before you can use it. You do this only once, and then the files will open from then on.
- An app on your Kindle Fire will open without any prompt and the file will be displayed.
- A prompt will appear and require you to choose an app because more than one app is available and capable of opening the file from your Kindle Fire.
- A popup will appear, stating the app is not a compatible file type, and then go away. The file will not open.

View Files in Quickoffice

If you tap a file that's compatible with Quickoffice, perhaps one you've downloaded, received as an attachment, or transferred via USB from your computer, Quickoffice will open and offer the file for viewing, or you'll be prompted to choose it if you have other compatible apps installed. If you've already saved the file to your Kindle Fire, you can open Quickoffice first and browse to the file to open it. Figure 9-7 shows the Quickoffice interface. Note there's Quickword, Quicksheet, and Quickpoint. Also notice the options to browse, search, and add accounts.

*Figure 9-7: **Quickoffice enables you to read Microsoft Word documents, Excel spreadsheets, and PowerPoint presentations.***

To view a file you've yet to save to your Kindle Fire in Quickoffice, in this example, one that arrives as an attachment via email:

1. Locate the file you want to open.
2. Tap **Open** as shown here.

Figure 9-8: *Quickoffice offers a few features, including the ability to have the document read to you.*

Although you may not be able to recognize that Quickoffice has opened, you can tap the Menu icon to verify it did. From there, you can also tap the Sound icon to have the document read to you. See Figure 9-8.

To view a file you've already downloaded or transferred to your Kindle Fire in Quickoffice:

1. From the Home screen, tap **Apps**.

2. Tap **Device**.

3. Tap **Quickoffice**.

4. If you don't see the screen shown in Figure 9-7, tap the up arrow (shown) and then the **Back** button (not shown) until you do.

5. If the file you want to open is:

    a. A Word document, tap **Quickword**.

    b. An Excel file, tap **Quicksheet**.

    c. A PowerPoint presentation, tap **Quickpoint**.

6. Tap **Internal Storage**.

7. Tap the **Download** folder. If you do not see the file in this folder, tap the **Back** button and try the **Documents** folder. If you transferred files via USB from your computer, tap the folder you saved to.

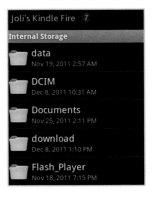

8. Tap the file you want to open. See Figure 9-9.

MANAGING SAVED FILES WITH QUICKOFFICE

As you've seen, you can access files that are stored on your Kindle Fire using Quickoffice. It's more than a way to view office documents though; it's also a way to locate and manage the data stored on it. For the most part, you'll manage data by creating folders and placing data there, renaming files, and deleting unnecessary data.

1. Open Quickoffice.

2. At the home screen, shown earlier in Figure 9-7, tap **Browse**.

3. Tap **Internal Storage**.

4. Select any folder in the list.

5. Place a check mark by any file you want to manage.

6. Tap the appropriate icon at the bottom of the page. For now, try the options to rename or delete.

7. Continue exploring as desired. Do not delete any files that you do not recognize.

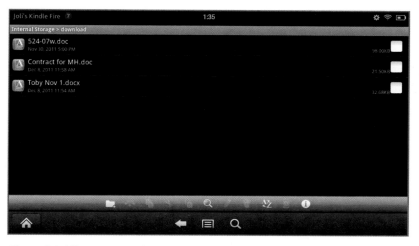

Figure 9-9: *Files you save from email attachments or download from the Internet are stored in the Download folder.*

Note the options that run across the bottom of the screen in Figure 9-9. Those options become available when you select one or more files in the window. Once selected, you can tap the related icons to create a new folder to hold files, share files, copy a file to the clipboard, and more. Figure 9-10 calls out the options.

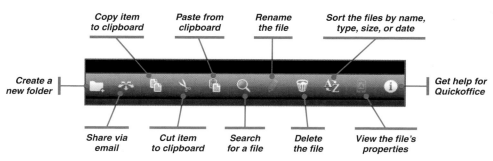

Figure 9-10: *Select files in a folder to manage them with the icons that become available.*

Incorporate Third-Party Accounts in Quickoffice

One of the options from the Quickoffice home screen is Accounts. If you tap Accounts, you will be able to add third-party accounts to Quickoffice. Once added, you'll be able to access the file stored in those accounts, provided you're connected to the Internet.

To add an account to Quickoffice:

1. From the Quickoffice home screen, tap **Accounts**.
2. Tap the account you want to add.

3. You may be prompted to accept terms of service or other notices. Tap **Continue** if applicable.
4. Tap your credentials for the account and tap **OK**.
5. Tap **Browse** at the Quickoffice home screen. Tap the account to access the documents in it.

TIP

If you tried out Google Docs earlier in this chapter and have an account, add it to Quickoffice for easier access.

NOTE

The version of Quickoffice that's installed on your Kindle Fire won't let you create documents, spreadsheets, and presentations. If you want all of the Quickoffice features, you'll need to upgrade to Quickoffice Pro.

Use Adobe Reader

If you haven't downloaded and installed Adobe Reader from the Appstore yet, you should. You can use it to open PDF files. Once installed, you use it like Quickoffice. You can either opt for it when opening a file, or open the app itself and browse to compatible files you've downloaded. Figure 9-11 shows the option to open a file with Adobe Reader.

To use Adobe Reader to open PDFs you've saved to your Kindle Fire, downloaded from the Internet, or transferred via USB cable, open the app first. From the app, you can easily select the file you want to open. Some files appear under Recently Viewed, not shown here, and the rest under Documents, shown.

Figure 9-11: **When Adobe Reader is installed, you can use it to open PDF files you receive in emails.**

Explore the Contacts App

There is one more app to explore in this chapter, the Contacts app. You can use it for business, pleasure, and travel. Like many other apps, it's integrated with the Email app. As you learned in Chapter 7, you can tap the + sign when composing an email and select the recipients from the list of contacts stored there.

You can also use the Contacts app to add new contacts, either by inputting the information manually or from a vCard you've received from someone you know (vCards are electronic business cards you receive as email attachments). You can also use the app to edit and delete contacts, or to simply obtain a phone number or street address.

Manage Contacts

The best way to learn about the Contacts app is to open and explore it. To see your options for managing contacts, you must first navigate to one.

1. From the Home screen, tap **Apps**.
2. Tap Device and tap **Contacts**.
3. Tap any contact in the list.
4. Tap the **Menu** icon to see the options (see Figure 9-12).

Figure 9-12: **The Contacts app offers a limited number of features, but does enable you to edit, delete, and share contacts easily.**

From the options shown:

- Tap the mail icon at the top of the page to send an email to the contact.
- Tap **Edit Contact** to add or change the available information. While editing, enter the desired information in the open fields and tap the **+** sign by any field to add more information. Tap **Save Changes** when you're finished.

- Tap **Share** to email the contact information.
- Tap **Delete Contact** to delete the entry.
- Tap **Search** to search for any entry.

You can also tap and hold any contact name to view these options and more. As shown here, when you tap and hold a contact, you can view it, add it to a list of favorites, edit it, delete it, or send an email.

| View contact |
| Add to favorites |
| Edit contact |
| Delete contact |
| Send email to : bryan@soda |

Travel with Your Kindle Fire

If you're planning on traveling with your Kindle Fire, there are a few things to know: how to keep your Kindle Fire safe, what accessories are the most useful, and what precautions you need to take and settings to configure while at an airport and on a plane.

Keep Your Kindle Fire Safe

There are ways to protect your Kindle Fire that you've already learned about. You learned in Chapter 1 how to create a password to protect it. You probably already know it's important to create hard-to-guess passwords for websites, and to vary the user names and passwords you use from site to site. Furthermore, you know you need to keep that list of passwords hidden from prying eyes. You may not have thought much beyond that though.

Here are a few other things to keep in mind:

- Don't leave your Kindle Fire unattended in a restaurant, coffee house, the deck of a ship, or on the bar at a ski lodge.
- Keep your Kindle Fire in your purse or a bag when moving it, if possible, to eliminate the possibility you'll drop it.
- Put the Kindle Fire in the trunk of the car, in the glove box, or under a floor mat (be careful not to step on it when you get back in) if you must leave it in the car.
- Purchase a case for the Kindle Fire that can protect it if you do accidentally drop it.

CONNECTING TO A PERSONAL HOTSPOT YOU CREATE

You may travel with a device that can be used to create a personal hotspot. This may be a smart phone, a tablet, or even a laptop. A personal hotspot is just like a "regular" hotspot to your Kindle Fire. You connect to it in the same manner. If you opt to do this, realize that any data used by your Kindle Fire counts toward your monthly limit on the device you used to set up the hotspot. To connect your Kindle Fire to a personal hotspot, tap the status bar, tap **Wi-Fi**, and tap the name of the connection.

CAUTION

If you are a believer in warranties, there's also a two-year warranty with accident protection from a company called Square Trade. If you opt for this, make sure to read the fine print as well as the reviews before you decide for sure.

- Try to avoid placing your Kindle Fire close to a cup of coffee or soda, just in case it is spilled.
- Make sure family members know the Kindle Fire is yours; if they want one, they can buy their own!

Purchase Additional Accessories

There are lots of accessories you can purchase to protect your Kindle Fire, most of which are screen protectors and cases. Screen protectors are thin plastic covers that adhere to your Kindle Fire's screen to keep it from being scratched. Cases come in all shapes and sizes and are used to protect the Kindle Fire when you aren't using it (and in some instances, even when you are) from spills, drops, and other accidents. These are two very good items to have.

Lots of other accessories are available, all of which can enhance your Kindle Fire experience. You can also purchase the following:

- **Ear buds**   Listen to media without disturbing others. Ear buds are very small and sit inside the ear canal.
- **Headphones**   Listen to media without disturbing others. Headphones are large and fit over the head and ears.
- **Portfolio cases**   Carry and use your Kindle Fire along with other items like a notepad, pen, stylus for your device, business cards, and the like.
- **Hard cases**   Protect your Kindle Fire from accidental spills and moisture, and prevent breakage should you drop it.
- **Sleeves, jackets, and skins**   Protect or decorate your Kindle Fire. Often, these are more decorative than protective, but every little bit of protection helps.
- **Stands**   Use the Kindle Fire hands-free. Stands are great for watching movies, listening to music, and using your Kindle Fire while you do other things.
- **USB car chargers, outlet chargers, rapid chargers, and power adapters**   Charge your Kindle Fire under a variety of circumstances.

TIP

There will be a lot of Kindle Fire accessories to choose from. As always, read the reviews and compare prices before making a decision.

TIP

You can download boarding passes for upcoming airline flights from various websites and using specific apps. You can save the boarding pass to your Kindle Fire, and at the security checkpoint, place your Kindle Fire under the security scanner to use it. You won't have to print your boarding pass if you do this.

- **Stylus**   Make selections on your Kindle Fire without using your finger to tap it. Instead, you use the stylus to tap the screen.

- **Reading, sync, and charge stands**   Hold, sync, and charge your Kindle Fire using a single unit that often connects to a computer.

- **Car headrest mounts**   Keep occupants of a car entertained on long car trips. Often, these hang over the back of the driver's or passenger's side head rests for occupants in the back seat.

Use Your Kindle Fire on a Plane

Everything you need to know about taking your Kindle Fire through airport security and using it on an airplane are the same as what you need to know when carrying a laptop. The Kindle Fire isn't a laptop, of course, but the airport views them all the same. Here are a few precautions to follow:

- At the airport, make sure you remove your Kindle Fire from its case, if you have it in one, and set it in its own container before pushing it through the luggage security scanner at the airport entrance. Occasionally, you'll be asked to power on a device, but not often.

- If you're going to pack your Kindle Fire inside luggage you plan to check, turn it off, and then make sure to position it in between several layers of soft clothing, and away from anything that could break or spill during transport.

- Keep your Kindle Fire in your possession at all times, unless you opt to check it in your luggage.

- Turn off Wi-Fi before boarding the plane.

The Kindle Fire Help pages say this about your Kindle Fire and airplanes: "If you need to turn off the Kindle completely, such as when traveling on an airplane, press and hold the power button for seven seconds until the screen goes blank." You'll need to do this during takeoff and landing. However, once the pilot tells you it's safe to use approved devices, you can turn your Kindle Fire back on and use it, provided Wi-Fi is disabled.

9

To turn off Wi-Fi:

1. Tap the Wi-Fi icon on the status bar.

2. Tap **Wi-Fi**.

3. Tap **Off**.

Chapter 10
Managing, Maintaining, and Troubleshooting Your Kindle Fire

In this chapter you'll learn how to manage your Amazon account. There's a lot you can do, including managing payment settings and configuring preferences for downloads, among other things. You'll also learn how to maintain and troubleshoot your Kindle Fire. You can prevent problems with proper management, and fix problems when things go awry.

Configure Preferences on Amazon.com

Because your Kindle Fire is so closely tied to your Amazon account, it's important you understand how to make changes to your account settings and configure preferences. You may be surprised to find as you explore Amazon's website that there are a slew of settings you can configure that affect not only your Kindle

TIP

The best thing you can do to protect your Kindle Fire is to configure a password to access it. See Chapter 1 for more information.

Fire, but also other devices you own. In fact, any device you've installed the Kindle app on can be managed somewhat from the Amazon website, as can any other Kindle model you've purchased.

Configure Your Amazon Account Preferences

Since you configure your account preferences from Amazon's website, it's best to configure those preferences from your computer, if you have one. The screen will be easier to see and options will be easier to access and configure. If you don't have a computer, you can use someone else's, or you can access the webpages and settings from your Kindle Fire using Amazon Silk. However, using your Kindle Fire instead of a computer to work through this section is more difficult because of the small screen; you'll have to do a lot of zooming in and out. There are two areas to manage: Your Digital Items and Your Account.

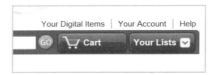

Click **Your Account** to view account options. You'll find there is almost an overwhelming amount of items to peruse. Figure 10-1 shows this. While it would be unproductive to detail every option you see here, in the next few sections you'll learn what you'll access most, and why.

ORDERS

TIP

From the Orders section, click **Manage Subscribe And Save Items**. Here you can learn how to select items you use regularly, order them, and have them delivered on a schedule. You may never have to shop for toothpaste again!

From the Orders section of Your Account on Amazon.com, you can view open orders (those yet to be delivered), view digital orders (items that have been delivered electronically), view Kindle orders (Kindle items), and manage your magazine subscriptions (to view, cancel, or see a list of magazines you've subscribed to). As with other sections, there are many more options, but this is a good start.

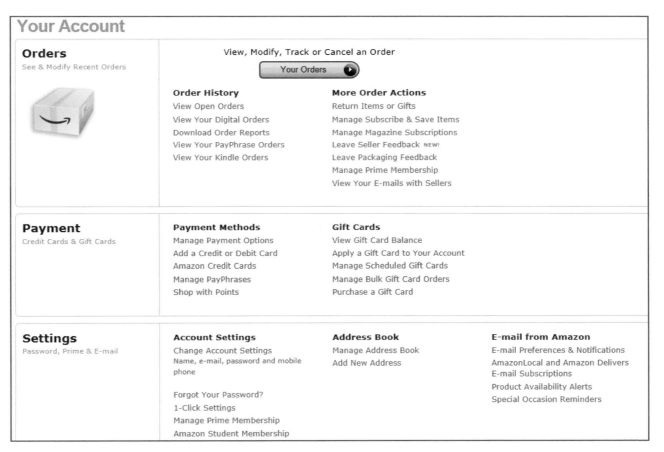

Your Account

Orders
See & Modify Recent Orders

View, Modify, Track or Cancel an Order

Your Orders ▶

Order History
View Open Orders
View Your Digital Orders
Download Order Reports
View Your PayPhrase Orders
View Your Kindle Orders

More Order Actions
Return Items or Gifts
Manage Subscribe & Save Items
Manage Magazine Subscriptions
Leave Seller Feedback NEW!
Leave Packaging Feedback
Manage Prime Membership
View Your E-mails with Sellers

Payment
Credit Cards & Gift Cards

Payment Methods
Manage Payment Options
Add a Credit or Debit Card
Amazon Credit Cards
Manage PayPhrases
Shop with Points

Gift Cards
View Gift Card Balance
Apply a Gift Card to Your Account
Manage Scheduled Gift Cards
Manage Bulk Gift Card Orders
Purchase a Gift Card

Settings
Password, Prime & E-mail

Account Settings
Change Account Settings
Name, e-mail, password and mobile
phone

Forgot Your Password?
1-Click Settings
Manage Prime Membership
Amazon Student Membership

Address Book
Manage Address Book
Add New Address

E-mail from Amazon
E-mail Preferences & Notifications
AmazonLocal and Amazon Delivers
E-mail Subscriptions
Product Availability Alerts
Special Occasion Reminders

Figure 10-1: Click Your Account to access this page, which offers access to more options than you likely ever imagined.

PAYMENT

This is where you input additional credit card information or update a card's expiration date, apply gift cards, and purchase gift cards, among other things. You can also delete payment methods here. You can even order gift cards on a schedule or in advance of an event, perhaps for outstanding employees of the month or for a spouse's upcoming birthday.

SETTINGS

In this section, you can change your email address, password, mobile phone number, 1-click settings, and join or cancel various memberships. One option is the Amazon Mom Membership, which allows you to get 20 percent off diapers, free 2-day shipping, and free 365-day returns on related items. It's a great way to have the items you need delivered to your door! If you're a student, check out the Amazon Student Membership. You can also add addresses here, if you would like to purchase gifts for others or have items delivered to a different address, such as one at work. And finally, if you think you get too much email from Amazon, opt out here.

E-mail Preferences
- Send HTML messages (pictures as well as text)
- Send mobile friendly messages (Mobile HTML if Available)
- Send text-only messages

Amazon.com Marketing E-mail
Note: even if you choose not to receive some marketing e-mails from orders, listings, updates about products or services you have purchase about programs you are enrolled in, such as Associates, Amazon Mom

- **Send me marketing e-mail from the following categories**

☑ Amazon Marketplace	☑ Computer & Accessories
☐ Amazon Partners ☑	☑ Electronics
☐ Associates ☑	☐ General Offers ☑
☐ Automotive	☐ Grocery
☐ Baby	☐ Health & Personal Care
☐ Beauty	☐ Home, Garden & Pets
☑ Books	☐ Industrial & Scientific
☐ Clothing & Accessories	☐ Jewelry

- **Do not send me marketing e-mail**
  Check this box to stop receiving all Amazon.com marketing communications (excep AmazonLocal and Amazon Delivers subscriptions, please click here.

[Save]

DIGITAL CONTENT

Much of what you can do in the Digital Content section you can also do if you click My Digital Items instead of Account Settings at the top of the page.

For the most part, managing your digital items means managing Your Cloud Drive, various media downloads, and your apps and devices, and accessing a list of games and software you've purchased. To learn more, skip to the next section, "Configure Your Digital Items Preferences."

PERSONALIZATION

This is where you configure your personal profile on Amazon. You'll want to do this if you write a lot of product reviews, or want to create a registry list for a wedding or baby shower. You can also access recommendations here, and do what's necessary to improve those. Finally, you can edit or delete your Amazon .com browsing history and configure advertising preferences.

Personalization Participation & Public Content	**Community** Your Public Profile Product Reviews Written By You Leave Seller Feedback Seller Feedback Submitted By You	**Lists** Baby Registry Wedding Registry Wish Lists Gift Idea Lists / Gift Organizer	**Recommendations** Recommended for You Improve Your Recommendations **Personalized Content** View and edit your browsing history Your Browsing History Settings Your Advertising Preferences

QUICKSTEPS

PLAYING MUSIC USING A WEB BROWSER

On Amazon.com, from Your Digital Orders, under Your Cloud Drive Music, you can access all of the music you have stored on Your Cloud Drive. Once there, you can opt to play any music through your web browser.

1. From Your Cloud Drive Music, use the categories on the left to filter your music. Consider **Songs**.

2. Tap the **Play** icon located either on the song or in the bottom-left corner to play it.

3. Tap **Pause** to stop playback.

Configure Your Digital Items Preferences

This section may seem a little dry, but it's important that you at least browse the Your Digital Items page of Amazon.com, if only to know what is available to you. Knowing what's there will enable you to better manage your Kindle Fire and your media in the long term.

From your computer (or from Amazon Silk):

1. Visit www.amazon.com, and if you're using Silk, make sure you're viewing the desktop version of the page.

2. Click **Your Digital Items**.

3. Notice the options, shown in Figure 10-2.

Your Digital Items

See digital products you've purchased from Amazon and music and files you've uploaded.

Kindle

Amazon's revolutionary wireless reading device. Read your Kindle books on your Kindle, PC, Mac, or mobile device. Shop Kindle Store

› Your Kindle Orders
› Manage Your Kindle

Amazon Instant Video

Instantly watch hit movies and TV shows, in HD, on your computer or on your TV. Shop Amazon Instant Video

› Your Video Library
› Prime Instant Videos

Amazon MP3 Store

Shop 18 million songs and find bestselling albums from $7.99 every day. Explore new releases and find fresh deals daily. Shop MP3 Music

› Your Cloud Drive Music
› Your Amazon MP3 Settings

Amazon Cloud Drive

Store your music, photos, videos and documents on Amazon's secure servers.

› Your Cloud Drive Files
› Manage Your Cloud Drive

Games & Software

The best way to get games and software. Instantly download thousands of titles. Shop Software Downloads or Shop Game Downloads

› Your Games & Software Library

Amazon Appstore for Android

Get a paid app for free every day and shop for apps using Amazon's trusted payment technology. Shop Amazon Appstore.

› Getting Started
› Your Apps & Devices

Figure 10-2: Your Digital Items offers various ways to manage your digital media, Your Cloud Drive, and more.

Click each entry on the Your Digital Items page to view what's available:

- **Your Kindle Orders** View your past Kindle orders by type, author, date, and more. In Figure 10-3, Books is selected.

- **Manage Your Kindle** View and then take an action regarding Kindle media. As shown in Figure 10-4, you can opt to deliver media (in this case, a magazine) to a specific device that can play or open it.

- **Your Video Library** View video you've purchased or access video you've rented (provided the rental is still available).

- **Prime Instant Videos** Access a list of videos available for play with a Prime Membership.

TIP

To cancel a magazine subscription, from the Action menu, select Cancel Subscription.

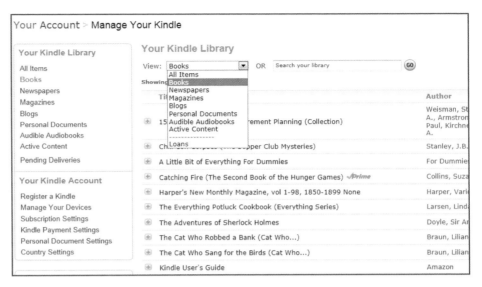

Figure 10-3: Choose how to sort your Kindle orders from the drop-down list here.

Figure 10-4: One of the actions you can perform is to download media to a Kindle-compatible device.

- **Your Cloud Drive Music** Access, sort, play, download, and otherwise manage the music stored in Your Cloud Drive. You can also create a playlist of music, and sync that playlist to your Kindle Fire.

- **Your Amazon MP3 Settings** By default, MP3s are stored in the cloud. If you'd rather have them automatically saved to your Kindle Fire, you can make that change here. You can also opt to download a copy of the song to your computer.

- **Your Cloud Drive Files** Access documents, pictures, music, video, and any other data you've uploaded to Your Cloud Drive.

- **Manage Your Cloud Drive** This area shows you how much of your designated free cloud storage you're using, and gives you the option to purchase more space if needed. You'll learn exactly how to buy more storage later in this chapter.

- **Your Games and Software Library** Click here to view the games you've purchased, as well as any software.

- **Your Apps and Devices** Here's where you can view a list of apps you've downloaded or purchased. From the Action menu, you can review an app, delete an app, and more.

Explore Additional Kindle Fire Settings

Throughout this book, you've learned how to access and configure various preferences and settings for built-in applications like Amazon Silk, Email, Video, and others. There are some hidden away, though, and a few you've yet to explore.

Explore More Menu Options

Almost all apps offer a Menu icon on the Options bar, and you can tap it to access the app's options. Often, those options include a Settings icon, as well as icons specific to the app itself. For instance (along with Settings), the Email app offers Contacts and Add Account; Amazon Silk offers Add Bookmark, Share Page, Find in Page, History, and Downloads; and Books (which does not offer a Settings option) offers options to go to the Cover, Table of Contents, Beginning, Location, and Sync to Furthest Page. Although you've likely seen all of these, you probably have not yet reviewed the Menu options for apps you use less often.

Because what's available from the Menu icon varies by app, your next step in exploring additional Menu options is to open an app you rarely use. To do this, open the app, and then simply tap the Menu icon and see what's there. As you do, you'll see both similarities and differences to apps you're more familiar with. Figure 10-5 shows the options for the Audible app.

Figure 10-5: Tap an app's Menu icon to access options specific to the app, such as Shop or Stats.

CAUTION

Although web-based apps such as Netflix and those you acquire for reading magazines do offer a Menu icon on the Options bar, at the present time, often nothing happens when you tap it.

CAUTION

Sometimes you won't be able to see the Options bar (and thus, the Menu icon) until you tap the upward-facing arrow at the bottom of the screen.

Third-party apps, those that aren't Amazon or Kindle Fire related, may offer menu features that you've never seen before. Here is the Night Clock app and options to set an alarm, change the color or font, or access advanced settings.

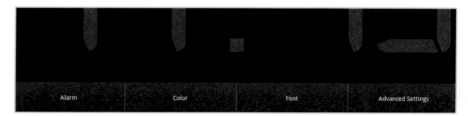

Explore More Settings

As you know, most apps offer a Settings option from the Menu icon. Tap it, and you may find only a handful of options or a dozen or more. Third-party apps may also offer an Advanced Settings option, as shown here for the Night Clock app mentioned earlier.

Throughout this book, you've explored the Settings options for all of the apps introduced. It'll be up to you to explore these options for the apps you own. To explore the Settings options for any app:

1. Open the app from the Home screen's Carousel, the Favorites list, or from the Apps section.

2. Tap the **Menu** icon.

3. Tap **Settings** or **Advanced Settings**, as applicable. Figure 10-6 shows that Settings is available from gReader, introduced in Chapter 9.

Figure 10-6: The Settings options for gReader include options to sync RSS feeds, read feeds offline, set preferences, and more.

4. Explore the options. You may need to tap to place a check mark in a setting to apply it or tap the item and make changes on the resulting screen.

Manage Storage

Your Kindle Fire can only store so much data. Some data takes up more space than other data. Apps and books take up the least amount of space, movies and videos take up the most, and songs are somewhere in between (although a song is more the size of a handful of books than a movie). You may also have pictures and other data stored on your Kindle Fire. You'll need to be mindful how much data is on your Kindle Fire at all times, and try to maintain enough free space to hold a last-minute movie purchase, to copy a must-have PDF from a computer at work, or to download the latest album by your favorite artist.

10

NOTE

Consider storing as much data as you can on Amazon's Cloud servers, and only keep data on your Kindle Fire you want to have with you all the time.

NOTE

No matter how careful you are, after a time, your Kindle Fire may still become full. When this happens, you must delete something.

TIP

Try to keep 1GB of free space available at all times on your Kindle Fire.

Remember: If you're away from a Wi-Fi network and can't access what's stored in the cloud, you can only access what's stored on your Kindle Fire. This makes it important to attempt to balance what you keep on your Kindle Fire and what you keep in the cloud. You may want to make sure you keep books you've yet to read on your device, perhaps a movie or two, your favorite apps, of course, documents you must have with you all the time, and your favorite music. You can always swap out the media when you're ready for a change.

Manage Your Kindle Fire's Device Storage

It may be hard for you to imagine how much you can store on your Kindle Fire at any given time. The actual amount of space you have access to and can use on your Kindle Fire is somewhere around 6GB. In terms of data, that's the equivalent of about 80 apps, plus 6,000 books or 800 songs or 10 movies. Consider that for a moment. Now consider this: as long as you never have more than, say, three or four movies on your Kindle Fire at any given time, and you're careful about the amount of music, home videos, and PDFs you copy, you should be able to manage the storage space you have fairly easily.

To see how much space is used and available on your Kindle Fire:

1. Tap the status bar near the Settings icon on the upper-right corner.
2. Tap **More**.
3. Scroll down, if applicable, and tap **Device**.
4. Review how much storage you have available.

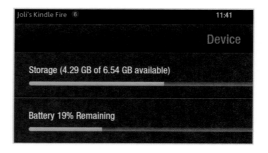

Delete Unwanted Data from Your Kindle Fire

If you're running out of space on your Kindle Fire, you should delete data on it. The first place to look for data to delete is under Video, and then under Device. You delete videos first because videos take up more space than anything else you will store. Figure 10-7 shows that Episode #23 of *Bones* has been downloaded to this Kindle Fire. Deleting downloaded movies and TV shows will free up a lot of data at once. If you need to delete more data, or if you don't have any videos stored on your Kindle Fire, move to home videos, music, PDF files, and books. You may also want to open Quickoffice, navigate to the Download folder, and delete items there.

Figure 10-7: Downloaded movies and TV shows take up the most space on your Kindle Fire.

To delete items from your Kindle Fire's Video Library:

1. From the Home screen tap **Video**.
2. Tap **Library**.
3. Tap **Device**.
4. Locate downloaded media you can delete and tap it once.
5. If necessary, scroll down to locate the title in any resulting list.
6. Tap and hold the arrow to the right of the title for a second. (You can also tap and hold the title name for a slightly different screen than what's shown here.)
7. Tap **Delete**, shown here, and repeat these steps as necessary.

After you've deleted downloaded movies and TV shows, check your Kindle's available space again. If you need to delete more data (or you don't have any videos stored on your Kindle Fire to delete), delete data in this order: home videos, music, and books. Although it's unlikely you'll still be storage-strapped after all of this, you can use Openoffice to find stray files like email attachments and the like.

To delete home videos or other data from the Gallery app:

1. From the Home screen, tap **Apps**, tap **Device**, and tap **Gallery**.

2. Tap **Video**. Alternatively, you can tap **Download** or **Pictures**.

3. Tap and hold any item you want to delete (see Figure 10-8).

4. Tap **Delete**.

Figure 10-8: A green check mark indicates the items selected for deletion.

To delete music:

1. From the Home screen, tap **Music**.

2. Tap **Device**.

3. Tap and hold any album or song.

4. Tap the appropriate "Remove" option from the resulting list.

A Decade of Hits

Add album to Now Playing

Add album to playlist

View artist

Shop artist in store

Remove album from device

To delete books:

1. From the Home screen, tap **Books**.
2. Tap **Device**.
3. Tap and hold any book you want to remove.
4. Tap **Remove From Device**.

One more option for deleting data, especially data you can't find in Video, Gallery, Music, or Books, is to open Quickoffice and browse the folders available there. To delete email attachments, documents, presentations, spreadsheets, and other saved data not available from other areas of your Kindle Fire:

1. From the Home screen, tap **Apps**.
2. Tap **Device**, and then tap **Quickoffice**.
3. If you see the Quickoffice introductory screen, tap **Browse**.
4. Tap **Internal Storage**.
5. Tap **Documents**.
6. Tap and hold any item you want to delete, and then tap **Delete**. PDF files can be quite large, so look for those.

When deleting data by browsing with Quickoffice, be extremely careful not to delete anything you don't recognize as something you created, saved, downloaded, or copied.

BUYING MORE CLOUD STORAGE

If you have access to Wi-Fi most of the time, you'll keep a lot of data in the cloud on Your Cloud Drive and Your Cloud Drive Music. If you run out of free storage space in the cloud (5GB), you can buy more storage space. Technically, you're renting the space, but that's not really important.

To buy more space:

1. Using any web browser, navigate to www.amazon .com.

2. Tap or click **Your Digital Items**.

3. Tap or click **Manage Your Cloud Drive** and log in.

4. Select a new storage plan and tap **Upgrade**. The least expensive plan is shown here.

| 20 GB | $20.00 / year | Less than $1.75 / month | Upgrade |
| | | **NEW** Includes unlimited space for music | |

5. Select your payment method and tap **Continue**.

6. Confirm and complete the payment process.

TIP

Data stored in the cloud can be accessed on any computer, simply by logging on to your account at Amazon and navigating to the saved files.

7. Repeat as desired, and then tap the **Back** button.

8. Tap the **Download** folder and delete items there using the same technique.

9. Repeat with other folders as desired, but only delete items you recognize.

Back Up Your Kindle Fire

When you make media purchases from Amazon and you opt to store those purchases in the cloud, your purchases are backed up automatically. If something happens to your Kindle Fire, you can still access anything stored there from another compatible device. If you get a new Kindle Fire, you can download it there too. There's really no need to back up this data yourself, but you still can if you like. That's what is so great about the cloud; Amazon backs up your purchased data for you. The same is true of data you've uploaded to Your Cloud Drive. That data is safe as well because it's stored on Amazon's servers, and likely your own computer too.

Data that you've copied from your computer to your Kindle Fire is also safe. That's because that data is already stored on your computer, so if something happens to your Kindle Fire, you can still recover it from there. You may have copied pictures, home videos, or music, for instance, or documents, spreadsheets, or presentations.

Data that you've received on your Kindle Fire and saved there, however, like a download from the Internet, an email attachment, or even a picture you copied from a webpage, probably isn't backed up anywhere else. This data is vulnerable. So are songs, albums, and other media you told Amazon to download directly to your device and not to store in the cloud. If your Kindle Fire is lost or stolen, you won't have any way to retrieve this data. The best way to back up data on your Kindle Fire is to connect it via USB to your computer or laptop, and copy the data over.

BACKING UP YOUR KINDLE FIRE TO A COMPUTER

Backing up data requires you to copy the data from one source and save it to another. You do not want to move the data. To make sure you back up your Kindle Fire's data correctly, follow these steps.

1. Connect your Kindle Fire to your computer with a compatible USB cable.

2. Navigate to your Kindle Fire from your computer as outlined in Chapter 1.

3. Select every folder in the Kindle window.

4. Right-click the data and choose **Copy**.

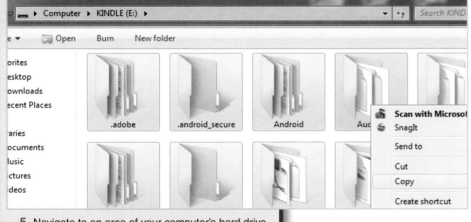

5. Navigate to an area of your computer's hard drive to save the backup copy.

6. Right-click and select **Paste**.

If you ever need to restore the data you back up to your Kindle Fire, perhaps a new Kindle Fire that is a replacement for one that was lost, broken, or stolen, you can copy the data one folder at a time, as applicable. Not all folders will need to be copied. You can redownload books, magazines, newspapers, music, video, apps, and Audible content, along with anything else stored in the cloud directly from Amazon. You may want to copy data from your Documents folder, as well as Pictures, Download, and a few others.

Troubleshoot Your Kindle Fire

You probably won't encounter any problems with your Kindle Fire, short of the occasional frozen app or a depleted battery, but issues have been known to occur. If problems do arise, the following sections offer a few ways to resolve them.

Know Common Problems and Solutions

There are a few fairly common problems that you may encounter as time passes. The screen may be frozen, the battery depleted, an app doesn't respond to touch, or a download won't complete. You may have trouble connecting to a Wi-Fi network, or have problems connecting to your computer. No matter what is wrong with your Kindle Fire, often a "hard reset" will resolve it. In layman's terms, this means forcing your Kindle Fire to turn off, even if it's unresponsive, and restart it. This is called a reboot. Whatever problem you're having, try this first. If rebooting your Kindle Fire doesn't work, completely charge the device, and then reboot it one more time.

QUICKSTEPS

REBOOTING YOUR KINDLE FIRE

To reboot your Kindle Fire:

1. Press and hold the power button for three seconds.

2. Tap **Shut Down**.

3. Wait for the Kindle Fire to completely shut down.

4. Press the power button again to restart it.

5. If the problem persists, plug the Kindle Fire into a working power outlet and fully charge it.

If this does not resolve the problem, or the problem is very specific, you'll have to work a little harder.

TIP

Make sure your Kindle Fire is up-to-date. Updates often resolve problems after the fact, or prevent them from happening in the first place.

NOTE

Your Kindle Fire can connect to open, WEP, WPA PSK, WPA2 PSK, WPA EAP, and WPA2 EAP encrypted networks. It can also connect to B, G, and N type routers as well as enterprise networks.

You can also check for updates to your Kindle Fire software from www.amazon.com/kindlesoftwareupdates. If an update is available, there will be instructions for installing it. (It's easier to follow the steps here, however.) Installing an available update may resolve whatever problem you're having. Although updates are "pushed" to your Kindle Fire automatically, if you've been out of range of a Wi-Fi network for a while or don't think you received an update you heard about, you can check for and update your Kindle Fire manually.

1. From the status bar, tap the **Settings** icon.

2. Tap **More**.

3. Tap **Device**.

4. Scroll down to **System Version**. If Update Your Kindle is lit up, tap it to install the available update.

If you're having trouble connecting to Wi-Fi, try manually adding the network connection, first making sure you're within range. You may have to move close to the wireless access device. If that doesn't work:

1. From the status bar, tap the **Settings** icon.

2. Tap **Wi-Fi**.

3. Ensure the **Wireless Networking** switch is in the On position. See Figure 10-9.

4. Scroll down and tap **Add A Network**.

5. Enter the name of the Wi-Fi network that you want to add.

6. Once the network name has been entered, tap the **Security** box and select the type of encryption the network uses.

7. If you select an encryption other than Open, tap the **Password** box.

8. Enter the Wi-Fi password or network key.

9. If you still can't connect to your own network, reboot your router and repeat these steps. Often, this resolves the problem.

CAUTION

If you've never been able to access your Kindle Fire from your computer, before connecting it again, power it on, use the slider to access the Home screen, and try again.

Figure 10-9: Wireless Networking must be set to On, first and foremost.

If you're having trouble connecting or accessing your Kindle Fire from your computer (and you've connected and accessed it before), first, disconnect the Kindle Fire from the computer, restart the computer, and then reconnect your Kindle Fire to it. Often, this resolves the problem. If it does not, and you're sure the USB cable isn't broken and is connected securely, try the following procedure.

1. Tap the status bar and pull downward.

2. Scroll to the bottom of the notifications list, if applicable.

3. If you see what's shown in Figure 10-10, tap it to enable the option to copy files.

Figure 10-10: You may see several notifications; look for the one about USB.

Finally, you can force an application to stop. To do this:

1. From the status bar, tap the **Settings** icon.
2. Tap **More**.
3. Tap **Applications**.
4. Tap the application that is not responding.
5. Tap **Force Stop**. See Figure 10-11.

Figure 10-11: You can cause any application to quit manually.

There are, of course, other problems you can run into, and there's no way to detail all of their solutions here. Besides, problems other than these aren't very common. That said, if you have encountered a problem that can't be resolved by rebooting and fully charging your Kindle Fire, you can get help from Amazon. Simply visit www.amazon.com, tap **Help**, and type <u>Kindle Fire Help</u> in the search window. From there, navigate to the area of help you need.

TIP

If your Kindle Fire is lost or stolen, deregister it from the Manage Your Kindle page at any computer connected to the Internet. In addition, cancel any subscriptions so you won't be billed.

Troubleshooting Your Kindle Fire

- Registration Issues
- Screen Issues
- Broken Screen or Case
- Wi-Fi Connection Issues
- Lost or Stolen Kindle Fire
- Connecting Via USB
- Password Issues
- Power Issues
- Newsstand Issues
- Books Issues
- Music Issues
- Video Issues
- Docs Issues
- Apps Issues
- Web Issues Using Amazon Silk
- Kindle Fire and Kindle Content Return Policies

Troubleshooting Your Kindle Fire

And finally, if you continue to have a problem you can't resolve, you can always call Amazon for help. Yes, you read that right! Here's how:

1. Visit Amazon.com and tap **Your Digital Items**.

2. Tap **Manage Your Kindle**.

3. Hover your mouse over **Kindle Help** and tap **Contact Us**.

4. Click **Contact Kindle Support**, and then click the Kindle Fire icon.

5. Make a selection from the list of problems.

6. Under Phone, tap **Call Us**.

7. Type in your phone number. Stay by the phone, and Amazon will call you!